The Life of (John) Conrad Weiser

The German Pioneer, Patriot, and Patron of Two Races

By Clement Zwingli Weiser

PANTIANOS
CLASSICS

Published by Pantianos Classics

ISBN-13: 978-1-78987-308-5

First published in 1899

Conrad Reiser's Grave

Near Womelsdorf, PA.

Contents

Appendix 70

Preface

There is no apology needed for writing the life of Conrad Weiser, if the opinions and wishes of knowing men carry with themselves any meaning or force. On the 13th day of November, 1793, General George Washington, accompanied by General Joseph Hiester and other distinguished men, stood at the grave of Conrad Weiser, and said: "This departed man rendered many services to his country, in a difficult period, *and posterity will not forget him.*" Richard Peters, Secretary of the Province of Pennsylvania, wrote already in 1761: "Since 1744 he has acted a prominent part between the Indians and the Government, by whom his loss will be severely felt. A faithful sketch of him by some of his descendants would be exceedingly interesting." Samuel Hazard, compiler and editor of "Pennsylvania Archives" and "Colonial Records," is careful to preserve the above remarks in his valuable collections. Thomas H. Burrows says: "On many occasions he was of the greatest service to the Province by his influence with the Indians." Franz Loeher, author of "The History and Fortunes of the Germans in America," speaks of his significance in these words: "One man, whose name figures so largely in the original records and events of his day, deserves special mention." Prof I. Daniel Rupp, the antiquarian and dweller among the *Manes,* has frequently revived his name in his numerous writings. Geo. F. Baer, Esq., of the Reading Bar, remarks in his address, delivered at the dedication of the new wing of Palatinate College, Myerstown, Pa., December 23, 1875, on the Pennsylvania Germans: "Then, too, the name and fame of Conrad Weiser, the great Indian Interpreter and peace-nmker, will be rcscncd from comparative obscurity, and he will be given the high rank and place in history which he so faithfully earned and so richly merits."

No student of our Colonial era need he told of the prominence of the man and his works. The wonder is, not that the links which compose his long and eventful history, should now be united in a chain; but that this service had not been done for him long ago.

The "Life of Conrad Weiser" is not a manufactured one. It is not invented, imagined or made up. It is no "baseless fabric of any airy vision" — no Hiawathian structure of poetical art — no arraying of an Enoch-Arden skeleton in fictitious flesh and blood; but the simple record of his life, as we find it enshrined in the facts, events and deeds of a long, steady, unostentatious and efficient course. It is but a reprint of an Autobiographical Journal, of parts of the Pennsylvania Archives, Colonial Records, the Hallische Nachrichten', the numerous Monographs of I. D. Rupp, and a gathering up of the floating traditions among his descendants, both in Peunsylvania and Wurtemberg. It is a presentation of the man, so far as this may be done, from his remains. The *manner* of its execution we must leave to the judgment of others. Were it but half as ably done as it was willingly done, then the work would verily be equal to the occasion. As it is, we can only pray the reviewer's kindness to take the hearty will for the imperfect deed. To the disappointed "descendant" of Conrad Weiser we feel like saying, "Go thou and do — better!"

C. Z. Weiser.

New Goshenhoppen, Pennsburg, Pa.
Centennial Year, May.

Introduction to Second Edition

No man has done more, and few as much, for the early settlers of the Colony of Pennsylvania than Conrad Weiser. Had he lived in New England, he would have been remembered long ago in marble, story and song; but, because he lived in Pennsylvania, he is forgotten even by his own people. The very grave in which he is buried is known to very few, and not decently kept. He and his wife lie buried in an old orchard on the farm once owned by him, near Womelsdorf, Berks county.

I started a movement in 1893 to begin to raise funds for the erection of a monument to his memory, as well as to protect the grave. This spot should be the shrine for every Pennsylvania German.

We devoted a period during the Berks County Teachers' Institute of that year to devise means and plans to launch the movement. It was resolved and agreed that the second day of November should be kept as "Conrad Weiser Day." Special exercises were held in every school in the county, suitable programs arranged and a contribution taken.

By these means we collected 8264, which sum is now deposited with the Pennsylvania Trust Company of Reading. It is hoped that ere long sufficient money will be raised to carry out this movement.

In our visitation of schools throughout the county frequent inquiries were made as to where books could be had containing information relative to the life and works of Conrad Weiser. To meet this want, the publisher of this book reluctantly consonted to issue another edition of the "Life of Conrad Weiser," and include in the same the most beautiful, yet pathetic Indian story ever written — the story of Regina Hartman, the German captive.

It is hoped that this book will find its way into many homes in Pennsylvania, and there arouse sufficient local pride, and love and respect for ancestry to complete the movement.

W. M. Zechman

Reading, Pa., September, 1899.

Life of (John) Conrad Weiser

Chapter One - Conrad Weiser's Remote Ancestry and Native Place

The first condition necessary to a fair understanding and correct appreciation of a character is to know his origin. Call it providence, destiny, fatality, no man can wholly escape from his ancestry, if we may credit that part of the Declaration of Sinai — "for I the Lord thy God am a jealons God, visiting the iniquity of the fathers upon the children unto the third and fourth generations of them that hate me, and showing mercy unto thousands of them that love me and keep my commandments."

In the ancient Electorate of Wurtemberg, also called the Duchy of Wurtemberg, a part of the once famous *Palatinate of the Rhine,* and in the town of Gross-Aspach, a place of some note in the county of Backnang — the pedigree of Conrad Weiser took its first beginning. "In this place," he tells us, in a fragment of his manuscript biography, "my ancestors, from time immemorial, were born and are buried — as well on my father's as on my mother's side."

The Lutheran Pastor Eisenhart, of Gross-Aspach, writes for us, February 17, 1871, from whose letter we extract as follows: "I herewith send you the Weiser Hneage from the earliest date within my reach. Our Church books extond back but to 1603. During that year the parsonage, together with some two hundred homes, was laid in ashes by the French. The records were accordingly destroyed. I may then ascend no higher, notwithstanding my anxiety to serve you. the *Pastor Loci* in 1697 epitomized, from memory and tradition, the names of all the surviving members of the congregation. On this roll the name of John Miehael Weiser appears, who died in 1721; and also that of John Conrad Weiser, who is designated a 'baker' in handicraft, as well as distinguished by the title of Corporal." [1] From the same source we learn that a certain Frederick Weiser, of the direct line, is at this time a resident of Gross-Aspach — a statement which a lately emigrated nephew confirms. We may also state, on written and verbal authority, that the name Weiser may be traced on the facade of an antique wine-press, which was regarded as one of the ancient landmarks of the place — in 1870, at all events. The patronymic is likewise engraved in the tablet of a venerable stone mansion, which either the historical Conrad's father or grandfather had erected. An eye-witness describes it as standing over from the Magistrate's office in Gross-Aspach. We were told that the stone had been carefully replaced during the rebuilding of the house in 1799.

Conrad's manuscript autobiography contains this note touching his forefathers: "My great-grandfather was Jacob Weiser, and my grandfather was, likewise, Jacob Weiser." The former he designates a "Schuldheisz," the Chief Magistrate of a district, somewhat beyond a Justice of the Peace among us. It is worthy of notice that the grandfather and father, as well as Conrad himself, filled the same office in their several days.

On the strength of Pastor Eisenhart's letter, Conrad Weiser's record, and the sayings of an eye-witness and living descendant, we are safe in regarding Gross-Aspach as the cradle-place of Conrad Weiser's ancestry, and that ancestry as of some age and honorable.

The numerous descendants of our venerable hero, scattered as they are over a number of states at this day, mav hereby learn the source-spring of their being. We know of no Weiser-scion in America, which is not an out-growth of Conrad, and through him a branch from the original trunk. This humble sketch will afford them the means, however spare, of knowing the quarter of their earthly origin, as well as the period of their forefa-ther's arrival in America, and line of their blood and name — all of which is fast proving a great satisfaction to the children of German, Swiss, French, English and other emigrated ancestry, in the measure according to which the society of our country is crystallizing into *families* — a pro-cess which no nation can eventually escape.

[1] The pastor alluded to bore the name of Hegele. He was subsequently deposed from the ministry for engaging in the very unclerical business of a wine mer-chant.

Chapter Two - Conrad Reiser's Parents, His Father and Mother

Conrad Reiser's father was John Conrad Weiser. He was born and reared in the town of his ancestry, Gross-Aspach. Following the humble trade of a baker in early life, he succeeded by difference and self-culture to attain to the position and office of "Schuldheisz," or American Esquire. He occupied, likewise, the station of a Corporal in the military service, and is so distinguished in the obituary note of his wife, which is entered on the necrological roll of his native place.

His wife, the mother of Conrad, was Anna Magdalena Uebele — not Webele, as it is usually written. This worthy woman was a native of the same place. We are told that the name is still worn by living representatives and descendants there.

On the first day of May, A. D. 1709, she died in the forty-third year of her life. The primal sorrow of her sex carried her from the bosom of her large family into eternity, when about to become the mother of her sixteenth child. Almost a moiety of this large group must have died quite young. Eisenhart informs us that only twelve names are enrolled, though in the mortuary notice it is distinctly mentioned in these words: *"Anna Magdalena Weiser died in the forty-third year of her life — the mother of sixteen children."*

The catalogue of surviving children, in 1710, runs thus: Catharine, Margaret, Magdalena, Sabina, Conrad, George Frederick, Christopher Frederick, Barbara and John Frederick. Seven of their children must, then, have preceded her to that unknown and silent shore, we feel constrained to add a tribute of regard over the ashes of such a "mother in Israel," in view of the bare but eloquent flict just told us. Is not such a woman a martyr in a certain sense? Her noted son, Conrad, had then boon in his thirteenth year, and tender enough never to have forgotten his early and great loss. He kindly writes of her: "She was much beloved by her neighbors and feared God. Her motto was, *'Jesus Christ!* For Thee I live; for Thee I die; living or dying, I am Thine.'"

Her religious nature was largely implanted and perpetuated in her son, as we shall more fully learn in these pages. The doctrine that ascribes all the noble qualities and virtue of a child to the mother is a false doctrine. Mind is not of the mother' exclusively. The children of the Indians are always distinguished by the name of the mother. The reason they give for this habit is, that their offering are indebted to the father for their souls, the invisible part of their being, and to the mother for their bodies. We are inclined to endorse their view as orthodox. The Scriptural argument in favor of its correctness can be conducted with ease, if we are permitted to quote the holy mystery of the incarnation as an analogy.

Yet the maternal influence counts for much, certainly — for one-half, if you please — in the formation of the offspring's character. This woman, though dying in midlife and when her son was but a child, lived on in him. Lilve a good angel, her piety cleaved close to his heroic spirit all through his eventful life. We must ever hold the child of religious parents at a premium.

Conrad could never cease regretting the loss of his mother. Any half-orphan, of any tcndrrness, will appreciate his feelings. You seem constantly to detect a sighing after her. This is an evidence of the availability of his nature, which even the savages could feel in later years. But might not that excellent mother's longer stay on earth have softened, weakened and enervated the child, and thus unfitted the man for the miles and

11

miles of marching, for the severe life that lay before him? May not such a silver lining he found to the dark cloud which so often empties its fatal charge on a household and strikes the mother?

Conrad's heart was of his mother, let us concede. But the strength, energy and self-reliance, which he exhibited, came by his father. Had not his father been just the cast-iron man he was, his offspring would never have shown so hardy a son. By Providence, then, the mother was suffered to come aloft, lest the son might be petted and indulged beneath the level, from which it is only possible to construct and elevate a hero. In more than one noble life may we find some such philosophy illustrated.

Chapter Three - The Exodus of Conrad Weiser's Father

"Is a bird that wandereth from her nest, so is a man that wandereth from his place." — (Prov. 27: 8.)

The man who is led forth by the demon of unrest, or mere love of adventure, from his country and kindred, will surely realize the truth of the wise man's words. God "had made of one blood all nations of men for to dwell on all the face of the earth; and hath determined the times afore appointed, *and the bounds of their habitations.*" This pregnant saying finds its application in the individual and family, no less than in the kindred, stock, tribe and race. It is in the violation of this Providential ordering that we may find the cause of the shipwreck of men and nations. There is a wedding of names to places, no less than a nativism of plants and animals.

But it was not from any such adventurous motive, we may safely say, that John Conrad Weiser, already beyond mid-life, left Europe; the Palatinate; the Duchy of Wurtemberg; Gross-Aspach; the dust of his ancestoi's that had been gathering and mouldering for several generations; the cradle-place of his being; his kindred and neighbors and friends — the like of which no man can ever hope to replace in the latter half of his history; his homestead, hallowed by the dearest associations and traditions; and the fresh tombs of his faithful and pious wife and little ones: all these for North America — the Wilderness of the New World — the Indian Territory of the Province of New York. Why then, was this Abrahamic Exodus? We may, to be sure, only surmise; but in this way, perhaps, approximate the true causes.

Europe was in a state of unrest. The Palatinate had been most cruelly visited and devastated by the French, especially in 1683 and 1693. Religions wars bore heavily on that once fair region. Spanish aggressions were followed by pestilence and famine. Finally came the winter of 1709, when birds perished on the wing, beasts in their lairs, and mortals fell dead in the way.

Why, then, continne to dwell in this fated place? Had not good Queen Anne, of England, offered a free passage to America, the fabled land of promise? Had not Hollanders, Swedes, Swiss; Lutherans, Reformed, Mennonites, Quakers, all these opened the way already since 1613? Could not Penn and Pastorius, and others, be trusted?

A migrating epidemic seized upon the stricken masses, and, as by a wave, 30,000 Germans washed along the shores of England. The Israelites were not more astounded at the armored carcasses of Egyptian soldiers lying by the banks of the Red Sea, the morning after their delivereranee, than were the English at this immense slide of humanity. A three-headed demon stared the realm of Queen Anne in the face — poverty, famine, war. Alarm set in. Riots ensued. How came the deliverance? Five chiefs of the Mohawk Indians, who constituted an embassage to the British government for the purpose of asking aid against French aggressions, saw and pitied — yes, pitied! — this perishing mass of men, women and children. They offered to open their hunting grounds lying beyond the great sea. The government, only too happy over such a prospective riddance, devised ways and means of transportation, and Robert Hunter, the Provincial Governor of New York, led 4000 Palatinates thitherward. "At the head of this colony," says the *Schwoebische Merkur und Kronik,* "stood John Conrad Weiser." National calamity drove him a voluntary exile abroad. Domestic atiliction, too, had but two months earlier embittered his cup. And may not, at certain intervals, along the line of history, the same impulses stir the bosoms of prophet-men or pivot-men as moved the ancient Chaldean shepherd to peril his all — not knowing whither he went.

Let us listen to the nearer details of the veritable uprooting of himself and his homestead, as given by the son: "In 1709 my father moved away from Gross-Aspach, on the 24th day of June, and took eight children with him. My eldest sister remained there with her husband, Conrad Boss, with whom she had two children. My father sold them his house, fields, meadows, vineyard and garden. But they could pay only 75 guldens; the remaining 600 guldens were to be paid at a subsequent period. As this was never done, it was made a present to them." A man at that period and in that country owning a homestead with adjoining fields, meadows, vineyard and garden worth 675 guldens, and titled, besides, as an Esquire and Corporal, he may well be considered to have been the leading spirit of the colony.

We will but add a morsel touching their voyage: "In about two months we reached London, in Knghmd, ahuig with several thousand Germans, whom Queen Anne, of glorious memory, had taken in charge and was furnishing with food." From the close of August until near the close of the year — four months — they fly over the Blackmoor. "About Christmas day mo embarked, and ten ship loads with ahout 4000 souls were sent to America." From a later notice we learn that this was a full six months' voyage. Considering the condition of this living freight, the rude construction of sailing vessels and the season of the year, we cannot well exaggerate the misery and suffering of our Palatinate forefathers. And yet Conrad, who having been but thirteen years old at the time, did not forget to magnify the kindness of Providence through a record in his private journal of this tenor: "Give thanks to the Lord, for His mercy endureth forever. Let the redeemed of the Lord say so, whom He hath redeemed? and gathered them out of the lands, east and west, north and south. They wandered in a solitary way. In the wilderness they found no city to dwell in. Hungry and thirsty, their souls fainted in them. Then they cried unto the Lord in their trouble, and He delivered them out of their distress!"

In what respect, we may ask, were the Puritans in advance of the Palatines? Neither in suffering nor in patience did the English excel the German pilgrims. We hail not the former less, but the latter more.

Chapter Four - Conrad's Father Chief of the Colony at Livingstone Manor

Queen Anne had directed, with the acquiescence of the benevolent Mohawk Chiefs, that the goodly tract, on which Newberg and New Windsor subsequently rose, should be granted by Letters Patent to the Palatines, as best adapted for the founding of their homes, schools and churches — the triune characteristic of our forefathers' advent. Robert Hunter, Governor of New York, and Robert Livingstone, a wealthy landlord of the province, however, knew too well how to hold the emigrants in suspense and delay the consummation of the good intention of the royal heart, until those grounds should fall under their own hands and control. They artfully and wickedly changed the course and destiny of the unsuspecting colony. Having anchored at New York on the 17th day of June, 1710, the conspirators removed the Germans to Livingstone Manor by the following autumn, with the malicious design of owning and possessing living property. Hardly had the locating been effected, ere they imposed an annual ground rent for ten acres on every separate family. Then $33 were exacted *per capita* as passage money. According to Franz

Loeher's calculation this taxation would have netted the sum of $200,000 for the men-mongers. Like the tasks which the Egyptian rulers imposed pon the Israelites, we may regard the burning of tar and the cultivation of hemp, which these greedy men exacted from the German colony at Livingstone Manor. Let us hear Conrad's own words, lest we might falsely charge: "Here, in Livingstone Manor, or, as it was called by the Governor, *Laebenstein's* Manor, we were to hnrn tar and cultivate hemp to defray the expenses incurred by Queen Anne in bringing us from Holland to England, and from England to America. We were directed by several Commissioners, viz.: John Cast, Henry Meyer and Richard Leykott, who were put in authority over us by Robert Hunter, Governor of New York." Who can refrain from recurring to the task-masters in Egypt? Did we but have access to their names, we might place them most appositely aside of their modern successors. Hunter and Livingstone were cousin-germans in the bargain and sale. The grounds were to have been a free gift, and their passage was to have been a free passage likewise. It was simply an outrage.

For a little while the colony toiled under the strange and galling yoke, rather than provoke the ire of their Pharaohs, in whose hands they found themselves, as clay in the potter's. But quietly a rebellion was brewing, and the soul of that rebellion was John Conrad Weiser, their Esquire and Corporal. To him had already been accorded the position of counsellor and leader during the voyage hither, and he now naturally led the movement of resistance, which resulted in the emancipation of the colony at Livingstone Manor in 1713.

Quite pathetic is his son's record in reference to this deliverance: "Many a time have they afflicted me from my youth, may Israel now say, and the Germans of New York; many a time have they afflicted me from my youth, yet they have not prevailed against me." — "They have ploughed upon my back; they made long furrows."

"Except the Lord build the house, they lalior in vain that build it." No pilgrim ever suffered more than the Palatinate pilgrims, nor with less blarney!

Chapter Five - Conrad's Father Chief of the Colony at Schoharie

The Palatines confidently believed themselves to be in near prospect of Schoharie Valley, the territory indicated and donated by Qneen Anne, at the suggestion and favor of the Mohawk Chiefs, who had witnessed their sad condition on the Blackmoors near London. Their sad discipline at Livingstone Manor dispelled their delusion. Then it was that they remembered the friendly Chiefs and their generous offer, with good Queen Anne's grant. Could not all those favors be revived? Deputies were sent to the Mohawks during the spring-tide of 1713. John Conrad Weiser was the first of seven deputies. Without awaiting the issue, the majority of the colony left their village homes along the Hudson. These villages were Palatinate, the Camp, Germantown, the German Flats, Tarbush, Ancram and Rheinbeck. Some strayed about in isolation, others sojourning at Albany and Schenectady — all awaiting a report from the deputies. In November the consent of the Indians was received. The valley was opened for their entrance for the consideration of $300. About one hundred and fifty families were consequently transferred to Schoharie, about forty English miles from Albany, in the spring of 1714. The sacrifice and toil incident to their second settling cannot be properly realized, even after reading the graphic recital of the junior Conrad, which we here insert: "In the spring of 1714 my father removed from Schenectady, where he had procured winter quarters for his family with a man of tho first rank of the Maqua Nation (Meinterstein), with about 150 families in great poverty. One borrowed a horse here, another there; also a cow and some harness. With these things they joined together, until being supplied, though poorly. They broke ground enough to plant corn for their own use the next year. But this year our hunger was hardly endurable. Many of our feasts were of wild potatoes (oehmanada) and ground beans (otagraquara), which grew in abundance. We cut mallow and picked juniper berries. If we were in need of meal, we were obliged to travel from thirty-five to forty miles and beg it on trust. One bushel was gotten here and one more there, sometimes after an absence from one's starving family for two or three days. With sorrowful hearts and tearful eyes the morsel was looked for — and often did not come at all."

And yet here an embryonic civilization was forming in the wilderness, which fruited in plenty and happiness. In the course of a few years the following villages sprang up: Gerlachsberg, Smithberg, Foxberg, Weisersberg, Brunnerberg, Hartmansberg and Upper Weisersberg. The names of the deputies were severally allotted to the settlements.

Given a spot of ground, with poverty and hunger to boot, and the German will turn the desert into a garden. This is characteristic of his nature, which we see exhibited almost daily.

The inner life of the settlement is shown us with a tinge of sarcasm in these words: "In those days there was no king in Israel, but every man did that which was right in his own eyes." Such a fellow-feeling renders men wondrous kind.

Chapter Six - Conrad Weiser's Father the Defender of the Rights and Liberties of His Countrymen at Schoharie

The story of Naboth's garden is a sad commentary on the covetousness of the human heart. There is this redeeming feature about the conduct of Ahab and Jezebel, though, that they offered an equivalent in money or another garden in exchange for it. This is more than can be said for Governor Robert Hunter and his mercenary coadjutors — the evil genii of the Germans. They permitted the unsophisticated and unsuspecting colony to remain in peaceful and prosperous possession of their newly acquired settlements, until their dwellings became homelike and attractive, their fields, meadows and gardens fruitful. Then, as the hawk pounces upon a dove-cote, these miserable, but powerful parties fell upon their victims. And these were some of their pretexts: The Germans' titles were defective; they had no proof of Queen Anne's grant; they had not flattered Governor Robert Hunter; the Provincial Governor had long before sold their fruitful valley to seven landlords: Robert Livingstone, Meyndert Schuyler, John Schuyler, Peter Van Brughen, George Clark, the Provincial Secretary, Doctor Steeds and Rip Van Dam. Surely these Germans must either fly or buy.

The singular and suspicions part of the whole transaction is that these are just *seven* landlords, one for every one of the seven settlements! In the language of the record "a great uproar arose both in Schoharie and Albany upon this notice." In vain did the terrified and perplexed Germans cry out against the injustice of sueh technicalities and fraud. Of what avail were the pleadings of the Queen's favor or the Indians' generosity? The ears and hearts of the voracious plunderers were deaf and dumb.

The Palatines determined to delegate three Connnissioners to London. These were *Weiser, Schaff* and *Walrath.*

The Governor and his crew, in order to gain time, plot more effectually, and, perhaps, wholly prevent the departure of the delegates, pretended to contemplate a favorable compromise. But suspicion and jealousy had now filled the minds of the Germans, and would not suffer them to brook delay. They secretly departed on their mission, at the expense of the colony, which was doubtless a burden for them to bear.

Already in Delaware Bay they fell into the clutches of pirates. Their private purses were delivered, but not the trust money of the colony. They were subjected to severe trials. Weiser was bastinated three different times, in order to induce him to disgorge. But he was too firm to yield.

Schaff told them they had their all, after which they were liberated without provision or suitable clothiug. They embarked a second time from Boston, after having begged or bought their outfit, and arrived in London poor, strange and helpless, only to find that good Queen Anne had died.

Hunter and company had likewise despatched their agents to England, who knew but too well how to misrepresent the Germans as rebels, as a pestiferous set and as enemies to the Crown. The German delegates were indicted and inprisoned for debt. They wrote for help, but their letters were intercepted. Finally the report of their sad lot reached the ears of their people at Schoharie, and money, gotten with sweat and toil, was forwarded — £70 for redemption. The affairs came before the "Lord's Commissioners of Trade and Plantations," too, and Governor Hunter was recalled. Walrath grew tired and embarked for home, but died at sea.

Nothing daunted, the remaining two petitioned anew, and succeeded at last in having an order issued to the newly commissioned Governor, William Burnet, to grant "vacant lands to all the Germans who had been sent to New York by the deceased Queen Anne."

In 1721 Schaff and Weiser had a quarrel. The former would no longer submit to Weiser's dictation, and returned. His son, Conrad, says: "*Sie hatten beide harte Koepfe.*" Six months after his return Schaff died.

John Conrad Weiser returned in 1723, after an absence of four years of suffering and sacrifice in the interest of the colony.

The new Governor felt like conciliation the disaffected parties, but they were nevertheless obliged to see their best acres abandoned or retained at enormous prices. Some made a virtue out of necessity and fell in with the new order, even at the expense of their manhood. Others would rather scatter here and there over the province. But Weiser could not trust any longer. Whilst his son was coming forward and assumed a conspicuous part, the elder could not fit himself into the existing circumstances. He quietly planned another exodus, which, though resulting in a failure for himself, as all his projects had proven since he left Gross-Aspach, was a happy enterprise for his son in the end.

Chapter Seven - Conrad's Father Leads a Colony to Tulpehocken, Pennsylvania. His Return and Wandering, His Visit to Tulpehocken. His Death.

About this time, 1723, His Excellency, William Keith, Baronet Governor of Pennsylvania, had been staying in Albany. Hearing of the unrest of the Germans in that province and anxious to draw them into his own, he lost no time to inform them of the freedom and justice that were accorded to their countrymen in Pennsylvania. It is even intimated that Governor Keith secretly meditated the founding of an independent state.

The manuscript record of the younger Conrad Weiser relates the following: "The people got news of the land on the Swatara and Tulpehocken, in Pennsylvania." Many of them united and cut a road from Schoharie to the Susquehanna river, carried their goods there and made canals, and floated down the river to the mouth of the Swatara, driving their cattle over land. This happened in the spring of the year 1723. From thence they came to Tulpehocken, and this was the origin of the settlement." A colony of some sixty families located principally in Heidelberg township. In the *Schwaebische Kronik,* March 8, 1868, it is asserted, on the authority of Fr. Kapp's "History of German Emigration to America," that John Conrad Weiser piloted this small colony to Tulpehocken, and that after a still further activity, during twenty more years, he died among his children and gnmdchildren in 1746. It seems that the opening and closing items of the relation are correct, whilst the important omission that he did not *remain* at Tulpehocken, leaves us under a wholly wrong impression. It has ever been a saying, on what authority we know not, that it had been his intention to commence the world anew on this theater. He came with the colony as a leader and pioneer, it was said. But the crowd proved too anarchical for him. Conrad wrote in 1745, whether with special or exclusive reference to this occasion we know not: "*Es war Niemand unter dem Volk, der es regieren konnte. Ein Jeder that, was er wollte, und ihr starker Eigensinn hat ihnen bis auf diese Stunde im Wege gestanden.*" His older children being married and settled in New York, it may be that he returned to his former territorv after a little while. Be this as it may, we know that he did not remain here.

"*Der Hallische Nachrichter,*" contains this item from the pen of the Patriarch Pastor Muhlenberg: "In the year 1746 came my wife's grandfather to my house; he had resided in New York since 1710, and lately on the borders of New England. He had left that country on account of the dangers which he apprehended from the French and Indians who had lately nuirdered several German families. Moreover, he was also anxious to see his children and grandchildren, to converse with them on the subject of religion and to spend his last days unmolestedly among his kindred in Pennsylvania. He was very infirm and frail when he came, and was confined in bed for some time after his arrival. After he had been somewhat convalescent, his son, Conrad, my father-in-law, who resided at Heidelberg, fifty miles off, sent a wagon with suitable bedding for them. He reached Heidelberg with much difficulty: lived but in short time afterwards with his son, and fell asleep in death in the presence of his weeping children and grandchildren." — (*Rupp's translation*.) His age is estimated at 86 years.

Thus ends the long, active life of John Conrad Weiser, *Senior*. After an almost unbroken pilgrimage of thirty-six years in the New World, he dies helpless and poor in the house of his son. One could wish him to have had greater success for his many and heavy sacrifices. A sterling, good man he showed himself to be. And, alas! so little fruit to enjoy. Was it the mistake of his lifetime to leave his country and kindred, at his age, and in his widowed state, wdth his large family of motherless children? Or, was he to be a forerunner to his son, who should thus have an open field to labor prepared for him? Or, again, did he but fly from evils which he knew, to lesser ones he knew not of?

His son finds the key to all his misfortunes in his ill-fated second marriage, as we shall presently see.

His remains are presumed to lie entombed in the graveyard adjoining the Tulpehocken church. The tomb, it seems, is no longer to be distinguished among the many in that locality. The Rev. Dr. C. H. Leinbach and son, and Louis A. Wollenweber, Esq., of Womelsdorf, have searched for it in vain, doubtless because a stone is wanting or its inscription proves no longer legible.

Chapter Eight - John Conrad Reiser, Junior. His Name — Birthplace — Baptism

It will doubtless create a surprise, bordering close on a protest, indeed, to be told at this late day that the prenomen, *John*, attaches properly to the historical Conrad Weiser — thus rendering him a full namesake of his father, John Conrad Weiser. Because he opens his autobiography in this wise: "I, Conrad Weiser, was born, etc."; and as he never, on any occasion, among the many that called forth his signature, records his name more largely, the public naturally took and tenaciously held to plain Conrad Weiser. Whether it was merely conventional, or in order to distinguish father and son, without dragging on the lubberly *affix, "Junior,"* we will not decide. But all discussion is cut short, and all doubt must vanish before the face of the Baptismal Record, which Pastor Eisenhart deciphered and forwarded. That reads: "John Conrad." The date and place of birth are, however, not noted with the entry of his name. This want Conrad supplies in his autobiography. He tells us that he was born at Afstaedt, which is a small village in Herrenberg, a county contiguous to that of Backnang, Wurtemberg, on the 2d day of November, A. D. 1696." He is careful, too, to note that he "was baptized in the church in Kueppingen, on

20

the 12th day of the same month and year. Kueppingen was the nearest church town to Afstaedt. Pastor Eisenhart had the goodness to address a letter of inquiry to the Rector at Kueppingen, and received the following reply: [1]

"**Royal Parsonage: Kueppingen.**

"In the baptismal Record of tins place, which also contains the hirth notices of Afstaedt, the name of Weiser is not to be discovered, whether ten years previous or ten years subsecpient to 1696. From your remarks I think this remarkable, indeed. With sincere regrets for not being able to serve you, and reciprocating most heartily your kind regards, I remain, very truly,

"Kueppingen, Feb. 15, 1871.   Pastor Eckstein."

Eisenhart says, in his letter: "I was especially anxious to know whether John Conrad Weiser, the elder, had not been a Chief Magistrate in Afstaedt, since he is so styled in the *Schwaebische Kronik und Merkur,* which I likewise enclose; though he is merely denominated a baker by trade, and a Corporol of the Blue Dragon, in the Records before me."

But whether we can account for the silence of the Record at Kueppingen or not, Conrad tells us all we need know in the words: "My father so informed me." This is, we may safely say, all the authority that most men have for believing that they were born and baptized in some certain place. His name appears on the Baptismal Record in Gross-Aspach as that of the fifth child born to John Conrad and Anna Magdalena Weiser, without date or place, as before mentioned. Eisenhart surmises the five eldest children to have been born at Afstaedt during the father's *temporary* residence there. An intelligent German informs us that government officials are accustomed to enter items of domestic history in the church books of their "Yater Stadt," no matter in what locality they may have transpired. It is fair to surmise, then, that the elder Conrad Weiser removed from Gross-Aspach, in Backnang, to Afstaedt, in the adjoining county of Herrenberg, discharging there the duties of his office until 1699, in which year we find him back again in GrossAspach, and the birth of his sixth child entered as occurring there.

The pietistic and biblical complexion of the man reveals itself throughout his Manuscript Journal, in the Scriptural selections which he appends to every paragraph. He crowns the entry of his nativity with such passages, to wit: "I will praise Thee, for I am fearfully and wonderfully made. Marvelous are Thy works; and that my sonl knoweth right well. My substance was not hid from Thee, when I was made in secret, and curiously wrought in the lowest parts of the earth. Thine eyes did see my substance yet being imperfect, and in Thy book all my members were written, which in continuance were fashioned when as yet there was none of them. How precious also are Thy thonghts unto me. O God, how great is the sum of them."

[1] The following letter Pastor Eisenhart had addressed to Pastor Eckstein:

"A clergyman in America, Pastor Weiser, who is a descendant of an old family of Gross-Aspach, some members of which emigrated to America in 1709, has respectfully asked me to furnish him with the records of his lineage as far back as it is possible to cull them from the church books, since he is minded to frame a Genealogical Tree, and to arrange the chain of his ancestors. I find, however, that one of the chief characters in line had resided in Afstaedt, viz: John Conrad Weiser, who is styled a Baker and Corporal; and his son, who is of the same name, and played a prominent part in America, it seems, was born there. And besides him, some of his brothers and sisters must have been born in Afstaedt, namely: Maria Catherine, Anna Margaret, Anna Magdelena, Maria Sabina— the fifth child would then be John Conrad. All these were born prior to 1699. During this year the family seems to have taken up its residence in this place again. I ask, accordingly, in case the church books extend back so far, to inform me of the dates of the births of the said children, and also of the title the father bears on the Baptismal Record. In the enclosed paper, in which the 'fata' of the Weiser family in America are mentioned, he is denominated a Chief Magistrate, though he is on the Record before me merely designated a Baker and Corporal. Had he perhaps been appointed to this higher position in Afstaedt?

"Whilst I, in advance, return my thanks for the desired contributions, and for the return of the enclosed slip, I embrace the opportunity, at the same time, of sending the warmest greetings of the inmates of the parsonage in Gross-Aspach, to the honored dwellers in the parsonage at Kueppingen, and on the score of old friendship, subscribe myself very respectfully,

"Your most obedient,

"Gross-Aspach, Feb. 10, 1871.   Pastor Eisenhart."

Chapter Nine - Conrad's arrival in America, his stay with the Maqua Indians

Conrad was nearing the close of his fourteenth year, when his father, a widower with eight children, landed at New York — three sisters being older, and three brothers and one sister younger than himself. About the close of November, 1713, a Chief of the Maqua Nation [1] — whom his father learned to know favorably, during his visit to Albany, on his mission of negotiation for Schoharie Valley — made a friendly stay in the family. This Chief was called Quagnant or Guinant. Manifesting a fondness for the lad, he besought the father's consent to take him to his own people. The elder Conrad, knowing the Chief as trustworthy, and the younger Conrad feeling no longer any home attraction, in consequence of his step-mother's entrance into the household, the strange request of Quagnant was acquiesced in.

Here we must, as we also happily may, allow him to tell his own experience: "I went accordingly, on my father's request. I endured a great deal of cold in my situation, and by spring my hunger surpassed the cold by much, although I had but poor clothing. On account of the scarcity of provision amongst the Indians, corn was then sold for five and six shillings a bushel, the Indians were oftentimes so intoxicated, that for fear of being murdered I secreted myself among the bushes."

It must not be overlooked that Conrad had by this time entered upon his seventeenth year. His stay continued during eight months, in which period the foundation to his future history and efficiency was well laid. Hunger, thirst, cold, lying in ambushes, entering on foot races and chases — courses in such exercises developed lungs, bone and muscle, without a bountiful supply of which the necessary endurance for his subsequent marches over trailing paths for miles and miles would never have come to him. Conrad Wciser had a call to a mission, and this Indian experience was the "college" in which his qualifications were developed.

Beside, Conrad Weiser during his eight months' tuition under Quagnant rendered himself familiar with Indian life — their manners, ways and habits; their instincts, likes and dislikes; their language — all of which constituted a higher order of education for his future work. This was civil-service-reform, however *un*civilized. We question whether the United States government, or any of our state governments, has ever had an official or public functionary wdio was better qualified for his post than Conrad Weiser proved. Perhaps when the world menders and government tinkers are all dead, statesmen will take a step backward, in order to get on in all matters pertaining to our Indian affairs.

Conrad Weiser proved an apt pupil under Chief Quagnant. Hear him tell: "During the latter end of July I returned again to my father's, from my Indian home. I had acquired a tolerable beginning, and, in fact, understood the greater part of the Maqua tongue."

He had at once occasion to apply his knowledge in this direction under the homestead roof: "About one English mile from my father's dwelling (at Schoharie) resided a few families of the Maqua tribe; and oftentimes a number of that Nation passed to and fro on their hunting expeditions. It frequently happened that disputes arose between the high-mettled Germans and members of this tawny Nation. On such occasions I was immediately sent for, to interpret for both parties. I had a good deal of business, but no pay. None of my people understood their language, excepting myself, and by much exertion I became perfect, considering my age and circumstances."

How rapidly did not this singular episode in the young man's life unfold its meaning! Providence indicated the open door. The Chief is an unconscious instrument in the employ of the higher motor. The farseeing and thoughtful father discerned and intelligently interpreted the fact. The youth voluntarily lends himself to this combination of circumstances. In eight short months Conrad Weiser is prepared to serve as benefactor to two races for a period of nearly fifty years — in a manner as Joseph served both the Israelites and the Egyptians. Do we not lose the emphasis and force, in a large measure, of Scriptural narrative by isolating those sacred incidents and contining God's remarkable interventions to a far remote period? Those holy relations are not written for after ages, because nothing similar had occurred before, perhaps, or will thereafter, but rather since they have a prophetic bearing upon the Redeemer of the world, in whose interest only "Holy Writ" has a concern. "I am the Lord, I change not." It is in this way that we may interpret many profane occurrences without becoming wicked. A profound student of the Bible is, perhaps, best qualified to become a historian. Is not Holy Writ a photograph of history? History does not repeat itself, but not so as to be a mere tautology.

[1] The Maquas were the Six Nations.

Chapter Ten - Conrad Weiser and His Step-Mother

When Conrad had attained to his fifteenth year, his step-mother entered the household, in 1711. We cannot tell her name. She was a German emigrant, and of the province of New York. We judge her to have been her husband's junior by much, since she survived him by many years. Her step-son does not speak kindly of her. We will let the reader judge from what has been already noted.

After his return from the Maqua tribe, a spell of sickness came over him in consequence, doubtless, of his change of living. This he relates, but not without reflecting severely on his father's second wife. "About this time I became very sick, and expected to die; and was willing to die, for my stepmother was indeed a stepmother to me. By her influence my father treated me very harshly. I had no friend, and had to bear hunger and cold. I had frequently, during my sickness, made my determination to desert from my father, after my recovery, but the bit of the bridle had been laid so tight to my mouth that I gave up this resolution. I was tied with a cord to prevent me from running away. I was severely chastised by my father, and finally took another resolution." This time, it seems, he executed his design, since we find him no later under his father's roof. We are sorry that Conrad Weiser left this portion of his manuscript record to remain. There is no excuse for him, aftor his experience with the Maqua Indians, and near his twentieth year, to thus reflect on his father's wife, and, through her, on his father, who certainly had proven himself a very worthy man.

The benevolence of biographers is infinite, it is said. This must be taken as a hyperbole, in the present instance. We do not feel like suffering his harsh words to pass unrebuked. It appears that every step-child feels itself fully licensed to berate its step-mother. By what style of exegesis a step-mother is excluded from the embrace of the first command with promise, we know not. Certain it is that step-mothers bear a very different reputation from that borne by step-fathers, or any parental characters of whatever sort. They, alas! constitute a race of women who have "no rights which we are bound to respect." From Conrad Weiser's unwise entry one feels like squatting them lower than the Maquas. And that a man, who proved himself so prudent and wise during a long and trying life, should have contributed anything towards strengthening this foolish and harmful prejudice, is to be regretted. We might excuse him for his imprudence on the score of youthfulness, had he but in maturer years recorded an explanatory clause. But even his son records her demise (1781) without erasing his cruel words.

The proverb runs: "A stepmother makes a stepfather." Perhaps, by extending our vision a little further back, we might learn that it is the *father* that is the occasion and cause of the stepmother, since he enjoys the prerogative of conducting her into the family. And once there, that father is as much bound to "protect" his second wife, or step-mother, even though it be against his own natural children, as he is required to shield her against any one's assaults. Whilst we would certainly expect such a father to consider duly his surroundings and relations, ere he leads any "strange woman" to his hearth and heart, yet, when the measured step has been taken, we will honor him all the more for asserting, in spirit and conduct, that he does not intend the spyder-and-fly philosophy to animate the life of his home.

We have a suspicion, from the manner in which Conrad entangles his father, that the elder Conrad Weiser intended to be master in his own house. It may be taken for granted, judging from his heroic conduct at Livingstone Manor and Schoharie, that he was fully able to conduct his family matters after an average rule of right. The younger Conrad, it may likewise be supposed, had become wilful, as it were, and free without becoming of age, and thus rendered the discipline of his father somewhat severe. The elder Weiser had come from a country in which the parents governed the children. Here is a picture of our Puritan ancestors, which applies equally well to our Palatinate forefathers:

"They were too stern, we acknowledge, and rigid; they knew little or nothing of the gentleness and sweetness of the gospel; but they maintained family government, and trained up their children to honor and obey their parents, to be honest and upright. Their sons grew up with strong and manly characters, patterned ai'ter their fathers, and tilled worthily their places, when they were gone, in the family, in society, in the church, and in the state. There is no use in denying it, private and public virtue was the rule; men and women, with rarely an exception, were loyal to their trusts, and could be relied on."

Such a man and lather we believe the elder Weiser to have been. And as Conrad was reared by him, and proved a true man, he is his own best refutation.

We know of step-mothers who excelled many natural mothers. Many of the former class, too, dare not venture half way up to the privileges and duties of their station, lest they be tabood by the children of their husbands, who are instigated and encouraged thereto by meddlesome neighbors and a vitiated public conscience. We are ready to affirm that many noble-hearted women have entered family groups of motherless children with the lofty motive and holy determination to be mothers indeed, who were, however, confronted by so fierce a prejudice against themselves, both within and without the homes, as to break down and die broken-hearted — and solely because they occupied the position in question. Either the practice of choosing step-mothers should cease on the part of wifeless fathers, or the said fathers should resolve to prove somewhat more valiant knights to the women who enter their castles at their own urgent entreaties. Then, it may be, the position of stepmother will no longer fall under par, because the character, conduct and spirit of *stepchildren* will stand at a higher premium.

Chapter Eleven - Conrad Weiser's Brothers and Sisters. His Occupation. His Marriage. His Departure for Pennsylvania

The motherless children of the elder Conrad Weiser had been separated and scattered over the province of New York already from the day of his second marriage, as the younger Conrad states. Having informed us that his eldest sister, Mrs. Boss, remained in the homestead in Gross-Aspach, he relates further that two of his brothers, George Frederick and Christopher Frederick, "were bound out, in 1711, by the Governor of New York, with the consent of my father, to a gentleman on Long Island." He speaks of another thus: "My youngest brother, John Frederick, died in about the sixth year of his life, during the month of December of the same year (1711), and was buried at Livingstone Manor, *'in the country,'* as the people called it. His tomb was the first by the spot where the Reformed church now stands." A sister became the wife of a Mr. Picket, whose son, John, Conrad subsequently recommended, in 1750, to the Mohawks, "as well suited to learn their language, and serve them after I should grow too old."

Conrad left his father's house during 1713-14 for an Indian town, about eight miles south of Schoharie. Here he resided until he left for Pennsylvania, in 1729. He was employed, like the vast majority of his German fellows, in agriculture under its rudest form. With only a limited education, but of an energetic and brave spirit, he filled the position of a schoolmaster, and thus, in the course of fifteen years, secured to himself a solid and useful self-culture, whilst he was teaching rudiments to his wards. Conrad Weiser was eminently a self-made man, so far as this is possible for one.

Here, too, Conrad Weiser opened his own family history. Of this event he speaks plainly: "In 1720, while my father was in England, I married my Anna Eve; and was given in marriage by Rev. John Frederick Haeger, Reformed clergyman, on the 22d of November, in my father's house, at Schoharie." [1] The maiden name of his wife we have never found mentioned; nor has any one else, so far as we could learn. Were we open to gossip, we might give full heed to the current and somewhat romantic tradition that Conrad Weiser had married a Mohawk Indian maiden. The invariable absence of her patronymic, coupled with the fact of his earlier and later residence among the Maqua people, constitutes the basis of the strange surmise. The fact or fancy that the immediate descendants of the pair had always been distinguished by straight raven-colored hair and a bronzed complexion, came in as an after-thought, and served as a very handy support to the view agoing. It was mooted, too, that the primitive name, *Eve,* was ominous of the conceived idea; and that it was designedly chosen, in order, on the one side, to ignore her former Indian origin, and, on the other, to indicate her incipient motherhood to a different race.

It is not well to fly in the face of an old creed, if it is in any wise supported by reasonable credentials. Nevertheless, we hesitate not to write down Mrs. Anna Eve Weiser as a full-blooded Palatine woman. It is easy to account for the rise and onward flow of the story of Conrad Weiser's Mohawk wife. His silence touching her patronymic made it necessary for his posterity to go in search of it. As Indians wear no family cognomen, the notion that she might have been an Indian lay nearer, and proved easier to harbor, than to successfully ferret out the lost name. The organ for marvelous conception, besides, is large in many; and nothing proves more attractive than Indian romance, in proportion to the distance exactly.

Whilst we cannot adduce a record, or any positive and direct testimony against the partially accepted Action, there is yet much strong circumstantial proof to the contrary, which mars and spoils the romance for us. Conceding the truth of the singular saying for a moment, how are we to account for the almost entire ignorance of the mother's vernacular, on the part of their *eldest* children, at least? Had it been indeed the mother-tongue of the household, then it is fair to suppose that the Mohawk dialect midit have become a family parlance more or less; and the older sons and daughters would naturally have taken it up in a measure. And yet, Samuel even is found to be too imperfectly acquainted with the Indian tongue to be efliciently employed by the government, in the room of his deceased father, after the fairest trial had been afforded him. His daughter, Mrs. Heintzelman, on the word of her father, "understood only here and there a word, from hearing the Indians talk at home." Nor has the learned world derived any contribution of Mohawk lore, even through the scholarly Muhlenberg line, though Mrs. Anna Maria Muhlenberg was Conrad Weiser's eldest daughter! In no child of the Indian interpreter has any knowledge of the supposed *mother*-tongue cropped out. Conrad had practically learned the Maqua language in his early youth, as we have seen, and had found an almost unbroken occasion to use it officially during a long life. This fact, of itself, would not warrant ns to expect even an acquaintance with a strange tongue, in the offspring, much less a familiarity. The language of court, government, or office, does not generally invade the precincts of the home. But let that tongue be the inherited one by the wife and mother, and flow from her lips, then the children wdll betray it, let them deny it never so persistently.

As for the straight, black hair and the dark hue of Conrad Weiser's immediate offspring, little stress should be laid on it. The stride between the premises and the conclusion is a fearfully long one. Thomas Corwin once said: "No man ought to be so impertinent as to allude to the Abolition theme in the presence of a man of my own complexion!" Still, Thomas Corwin's mother was not an Indian woman. It would, indeed, prove a difficult task to find a sufficient number of Indian maidens to mother all the offspring of sombre, tawny hue. A hair is a slender thing to run a distinction on, and a shade is a fickle thing.

The fact that the Indians characterized Conrad Weiser as "one-half a Seven Nation Indian and one-half an Englishman," seems to support the romantic theory. But even this double claim is satisfied by the circumstances of his birth and adoption. It is ever so interpreted and explained

28

by the responses of the different Governors and officials, in councils and conferences. Besides, his fellow interpreter, Shekallamy, an Indian, is spoken of in like terms, who certainly had not been wedded to a white woman.

A much more likely explanation for the absence of Anna Eve's family name is that she had been an indentured orphan girl, whose parents had either died during her early infancy, or whose parentage had been ignored in consequence of her indentured condition. Such an accident befell the young not seldom, during the unorganized and unfixed state of society, of her maiden days. The lot of the "redemptioner" was a sad lot in more than one respect. We have heard it said that Conrad Weiser called his bride "My Anna Eve," for the very good reason that neither he nor she could tell what more to call her.

We, therefore, call for the record. And until that is produced, or its equavalent, we will permit John Rolfe, the handsome English planter of Virginia, to remain alone in the glory of having won and wedded the Indian maiden, Pochahontas — however inviting a basis the low whisper affords him to build his romance upon, who prides himself over the imaginary Indian blood coursing through his veins. *(See note, next page.)*

Here four of his children were born — Philip, Frederick, Anna Maria and Madlina.

Aside of his domestic calling, as farmer and pedagogue, he had acquired some skill as a lapidary. There is in our possession a stone handle to a riding-whip, which our forefathers have ever highly prized and carefully secnred, because it was the workmanship of Conrad Weiser. It is of an octagonal form, and very high polish. This, with a large mirror and a heavy silver spoon, constitutes our whole collection of souvenirs of the man, though other members of his line, it is said, retain a larger and rarer cabinet.

During his father's absence in England, and after 1723, Conrad seems to have taken a conspicuous place in Provincial affairs. Familiar with the Mohawk tongue, be stood between the Indians and the English, as well as between the English and the Germans, in all matters oi intercourse or dispute; whilst the active part his sire had taken during his active life at Livingstone and Schoharie had initiated him early into the secret of shielding his own countrymen against the tricks and encroachments of government officials. "In the commencement of the year 1721," says he, "I was sent with a petition to the newly arrived Governor Burnet." In such like transactions he bore a diligent hand for about a decade of years, when he left the province.

[1] The colony extended along both sides of the Hudson. Pastor John Frederick Haeger officiated on one side, and Pastor Joshua Koeherthaler on the other.

[2] We find the following extract recorded in an old family Bible, which we insert here, without being able, however, to vouch for its correctness:

"Rev. Mr. Muhlenberg, likewise, writes in the *Hallische Nachrichten:* 'Our young interpreter remained back and entered into matrimony with a German Christian maiden, of Evangelical parentage, in 1720.'"

Chapter Twelve - Conrad Weiser's Advent in Pennsylvania, the Beginning of his Official History

Six years after his father's pioneer visit to this province, at the head of a colony of perhaps sixty families, and nine years after his marriage, Conrad Weiser arrived at Tulpehocken, being now thirty-three years old. We are not left in doubt as to the time and place of his advent. "In 1729 I removed to Pennsylvania and settled at Tulpehocken." Here, in this valley, in the township of Heidelberg — named after a city in south Germany, in the duchy of Baden — one-half mile east of the town of Womelsdorf, he located his permanent residence, in the year when Independence Hall was commenced. His chief aim was to be a farmer, as we infer, both from his own later declarations and the extent of agricultural acres which gradually came into his possession — numbering nearly one thousand acres, during a period of thirty years. But the circumstances of the country at that time and the peculiar qualifications of the man did not afford him such seclusion. There is a divinity in the affairs of men, communities and things which manifests itself in the law of demand and supply — in that law of compensation which provides organs and agents for every legitimate emergency. The intermingling of Indians, English and German people challenged the presence and service of just such a mail, as a solution to the complication of circumstances. And here again was fulfilled that saying, "There standeth one among you."

Conrad Weiser first appears in the charaeter of a volunteer interpreter for the Couneil of Pennsylvania and several Indians. Shekallamy [1] finds him, already in 1731, in the wilds of Tulpehoeken, and prevails on him to aecompany him to Philadelphia. Here Governor Gordon, likely, learned to know and appreciate him. The sum of forty shillings was accorded him on this occasion for his free-will services. Under date of December, 1731, we find the following entry made in the account of the Provincial Treasurer: "To cash, by order of the Board, paid to Conrad Weiser, who, at Shekallamy's desire, attended him from Tulpehocken, £2, 11s." After this introduction he remains continually in the public eye. A like order to the one just mentioned is recorded as having been honored March, 1732, for £3, 13s., 5d., for services rendered to the Shawnese Indians and the province.

But the way was now opening for a more public and significant station. In the month of August, 1732, the Six Nations [2] express themselves as "very desirous that there may be more frequent opportunities of conferring and discoursing with their brothers, and that these may be managed by the means of Shekalhimy and Conrad Weiser." On the following day the Indians say that "they would be pleased to have an answer to their prnposition." The Governor replied as follows: "As to what you have said about employing Shekallamy and Council Weiser, on which you gave the first strings of Wampum, [3] we are very glad you agree with us in the choice of so good men to go between us. We believe them to be very honest, and will with cheerfulness employ them." The Council then presented the sum of £12 to Conrad Weiser "for accompanying and being very careful of the Indians on their way from Tulpehocken; and for having been extremely useful in framing an initiatory treaty with them." It is also said, to the honor of the man, that "because the men were not only very acceptable to the Indians, as appeared by their late recommendation of them, but likewise seemed to be persons of truth and honesty, all due encouragement should be given them." Having thus secured the good will of the Provincial Officials and Indian Chiefs, by his native excellence and faithfulness, he is the acceptable mediator, henceforth, between the waxine and waning races. Conrad Weiser, accordingly, in the course of three years, steps out of his Tulpehocken obscurity into the position of an official and historical character.

William Penn and Conrad Weiser are two men, at least, of whom the Indians think and speak well. It is not too much to say that the pacific spirit of Penn was perpetuated by Weiser, and that the fair name of our Commonwealth, touching our treatment of the Indians, is perhaps as much owing to the fine policy of the latter as it is to the amiable mind of the former.

[1] Shekallamy was an agent for the Five or Six Nations, and resided at Shamokin. He is spoken of "as a trusty and good man, and a great lover of the English." In 1756, on Feb. 24, his son spoke in these words concerning him, in Philadelphia: "My father, who, it is well known, was all his life a hearty and steady friend to the English, and to this province in particular, charged his children to follow his steps and to remain always true to the English, who had been ever kind to him and his family."

[2] The "Four," "Five" and "Six Nations" were an Indian Union, formed by the following tribes: M aqua (Mohawks), Onondagos, Senekas, Oneydas, Tuskaroras, Cayoogas, Conrad Weiser says these lived from 200 to 500 miles from Lancaster, Pa. They are spoken of as the Iroquois, and for the most part dwelt in the northern portion of the United States— near the great laken, in New York, etc. Onondago was their Council Ground, whither the delegates came annually or semi-

annually to deliberate on general affairs. Their conventions were said to have been quite edifying.

[3] A Belt of Wampum is a leathern string, on which are threaded white and violet shells, which are found on the coasts of New England and Virginia, and are cut into beads of an oblong form. It is a very solemn instrument among the Indians, as well as an ornamental wearing. It signifies a league of friendship, a ratification, a mark of honor, etc.

Chapter Thirteen - Conrad Weiser Provincial Interpreter, Justice of the Peace - 1732-1743

From the year 1732, when George Washincrton was born, we may regard Conrad Weiser the officially recognized interpreter of Pennsylvania. President Logan says, October 12, 1736: "Conrad Weiser and Shekallamy were, by the treaty of 1732, appointed fit and proper persons to go between the Six Nations and this government, and to be employed in all transactions with one another; "whose bodies," the Indians say, "were to be equally divided between them and us, we to have one-half and they the other." They say "they have always found Conrad faithful and honest. He is a good and true man, and has spoken their words and our words — not his own." The Indians have presented him with a dressed skin to make him shoes, and two deer skins to keep him warm."

The provinces of Virginia, Maryland and New York employed him in a like capacity, somewhat later. On the side of the Indians all Tribes and Nations engaged him, and there was no important negotiation transacted, involving the interests of both races, in which he was not made use of. Durino; the interval between 1732 and 1736 the messengers of the Six Nations were constantly pasing to and fro, in order to bring the treaty to a ratification. Conrad Weiser is the pivot man on all such occasions. Shekallamy naively says, in 1734, when not finding his trusty friend on hand: "Having finished inquiry, I will go to see Conrad Weiser, at Tulpehocken, and either relate it to him to be sent down hither in writing, or, if it be found to be of consequence, I will come hither and deliver it myself."

In 1735 he made a religious somersault, which will be noticed hereafter.

The Council minutes, as they are preserved for us in the Colonial Records and Pennsylvania Archives, frequently record his name, at short intervals, over a dozen or more pages. Notice is taken of his valuable services, both by the Indians and the Council, again and again, and always in most favorable terms. In September, 1736, the Chiefs of the Six Nations were expected in Philadelphia to confirm the treaty of 1732. He informed the Council, from Tulpehocken, that a large number would arrive from Shamokin, on the Susquehanna, and was asked to repair to Philadelphia at once, to attend and provide for them. On the 27th the Chiefs, with Weiser, came to the President's house at Stenton. Here a feast was provided. On the 28th the Council was held, in the presence of Governor Thomas Penn, the Chiefs and other dignitaries. Conrad Weiser the Indians style "our friend." The sum of £20 is awarded him, and in no grudging way, as may be gathered from the following extract: "He has been very serviceable — which sum the Provincial Treasurer is directed to pay, and that he advance the said sum."

When Governor Gooch, of Virginia, desired this province to mediate between the Six Nations, the Cherokees, the Catawbas and others, and himself, Logan writes thus: "I had an opportunity of seeing Conrad Weiser, and judging him, from the experience this goverumcnt has had of his honesty and fidelity, to be the most proper person to carry the Six Nations the proposed message in this letter, I engaged Weiser to undertake the business, and gave him proper instructions to that end. He, now being returned, has, in his own words and handwriting, given a very distinct and satisfactory account of the errand he was sent on; the Board will find it, in substance, to signify that the Six Nations are ready and willing to treat of and conclude a peace with their enemies; but declining to go to Williamsburg, they propose Albany."

In 1737 he was accordingly sent to Onondago, N. Y. This was his first great mission. He leaves Tulpehocken in February for a journey some five hundred miles long, through a wilderness without road or path, in the face of danger. His experiences are well told in his Journal, to which the reader is referred. In all the following years his name occurs on many pages, as though he were the most prominent man of the day. We question, too, whether any one man had been more widclv and more favorably known, at that period, than Conrad Weiser was. It would tire our hand to write and but weary the eye, were we faithfully to insert this entry — "Conrad Weiser, interpreter" — as often as it is made to stand on the official record.

During the year 1738, in May, he accompanies Bishop Spangenberger, David Zeisberger and Shebosch, Moravian missionaries to the Indians, to Onondago again. Their hardships were many and great, all of which he cheerfnlly and heroically endured.

But he was not unmindful of home interests, thongh, as it seems, so constantly engaged abroad. We never found a man busier over a larger territory, without neglecting his own house and neighborhood. In 1739-40, February 4, he saw the propriety of organizing a new county, and accordingly signs a prayer to that effect, though the county of Berks did not come forth till 1752.

In the year 1741 he was commissioned as a Justice of the Peace for Lancaster county, and thus succeeded to the office which his father and grandfather had filled in Gross-Aspach. He continued in service as a Justice for many years, and after the erection of Berks county he filled it within that territory, likewise. Fr. Loeher speaks of him as a Magistrate "known far and wide as an upright officer." But he displeased the lawless on many occasions, for be it remembered, Conrad Weiser was a *religious* man. Of a certain family he complains woefully, and thinks them "worse than any Indian or Frenchman." He acknowledges that he stands in dread of the members of the household. And well he might. One night those upon whom he pronounced the law's penalty, barred his windows and blockaded the doors, setting fire to some straw and other combustibles which they had carried under the stoop. One of the children awoke and gave the alarm. They broke through a window and thus escaped being burned alive.

It is related, as showing the humor of the man, that a certain troublesome woman, who had been continually worrying him for the arrest of her husband on the charge of "assault and battery," was once asked by him whether she did not sometimes deserve a little castigation at her husband's hands? To this query the woman, after some hesitation, made answer that she believed it to be his right and her profit to have a chastisement administered occasionally, but that he indulged too frequently and too severely in the discipline.

In July, 1742, an account of his expenses was exhibited, amounting to £36, 18s., 3d. This seems a large bill; but that it did not strike the officials as being too exorbitant, or as calling for an investigation, the extract which we insert will show: "Taking into consideration the many signal services performed by Conrad Weiser to this Government, his diligence and labor in the service thereof, and his skill in the Indian languages and methods of business, we are of the opinion that the said Conrad should be allowed, as a reward from this Province, at this time, the sum of thirty pounds at least, besides payment of his said account."

Cannassatego, a Delaware Chief, bespeaks the good will of the Council at Philadelphia after this manner, in his behalf: "Ye esteem our present Interpreter to bo such a person, equally faithful in the interpretation of whatever is said to him, by either of us; equally allied to both. He is of our Nation and a member of our Council, as well as of yours. When we adopted him, we divided him into two equal parts — one-half we kept for ourselves and one-half we kept for you. He has a great deal of trouble with us. He wore out his shoes in our messages and dirtied his clothes by being among us, so that he is as nasty as an Indian. In return for these services we recommend him to your generosity. And in our own behalf we gave him five skins to buy him clothes and shoes with."

The Hon. George Thomas, Lieut. Governor of the province, replied in these words: "We entertain the same sentiments of the abilities and probity of the interpreter as yon have expressed. We were induced, at first, to make use of him in this important trust, from his being known to be agreeable to you, and one who had lived amongst you for some years in good credit and esteem with all your Nation, and have ever found him equally faithful to both. We are pleased with your notice of him, and think he richly deserves it at your hands. We shall not be wanting to make him a suitable gratification for the many good and faithful services he has done this government."

It was in this year, during the month of July (12th), that another Tribe ratified the deed, given some years earlier, for the land along the Schuylkill. To this instrument the names of Benjamin Franklin and Conrad Weiser are appended.

But another important mission opened before him. Count Zinzendorf had arrived in America, and was anxious that Conrad Weiser should accompany him to Bethlehem, to preach to the Indians. There he, accordingly, interpreted for the Count during the month of August. "This is the man," said he, "whom God hath sent, both to the Indians and the white people, to make known His will to them." On a similar errand he accompanied Count Zinzendorf, shortly afterwards, to Shamokin. He was enraptured over the success of the gospel among the Indians. He expresses his delight in a letter, from which we cull the following extracts:

"I was very sorry not to have seen you at Shamokin (Buettner), owing to your indisposition. But the pleasure I felt, during my abode there, left a deep impression upon me. The faith of the Indians in our Lord Jesus Christ — their simplicity and unaffected deportment; their experience of the grace procured for us by the sufferings of Jesus, preached to them by the brethren — has impressed my mind with a firm belief that God is with you. I thought myself seated in a company of primitive Christians.

"The old men sat partly upon benches and partly upon the ground, for want of room, with great gravity and devotion, their eyes steadfastly fixed upon their teacher, as if they would eat his words. John was the interpreter, and acquitted himself in the best manner. I esteem him as a man anointed with grace and spirit. Though I am not well acquainted with the Matikander language, yet their peculiar manner of delivery renders their ideas intelligible to me as to any European in this country. In short, I deem it one of the greatest favors bestowed upon me in this life that I have been at Shamokin.

"That text of Scripture, 'Jesus Christ the same yesterday and to-day, and forever,' appeared to me as an eternal truth when I beheld the venerable patriarchs of the American Indian Church sitting around me, as living witnesses of the power of our Lord Jesus Christ and of His atoning sacri-

35

fice. Their prayers are had in remembrance in the sight of God — and may God fight against their enemies. May the Almighty God give to you and your assistants an open door to the hearts of all the heathens. This is the most earnest wish of your sincere friend,   Conrad Weiser."

However sanguine he may have been of the conversion of the Indians, at the time of his writing, we do not find that he colleague longer with the Moravian missionarics in prosecuting the noble undertaking. This much credit must, nevertheless, be given him that he at that early day suggested the only true plan by which any missionary work can ever be carried forward, whether the material to be evangelized be Indian, African, or Asian or European. Pastor Muhlenberg states it in these words: "Mr. Weiser is of the opinion that to convert them to Christianity it would be essential, among other methods, to adopt something like the following:

"I. Several missionaries should take up their abode in the midst of the Indians and strive to make themselves thorough masters of their language; conform as far as possible to their costumes, manners and customs, yet reprove their natural vices by a holy, meek and virtuous deportment.

"II. Translate Revealed Truth into their own language, and present the whole as intelligibly as possible.

"III. The missionaries should study the Indian tunes and melodies, and convey to them the law and the Gospel, in such tunes and melodies, in order to make an abiding impression, and thereby, under the blessing and increase of God, patiently wait for the fruits of their labors." — (*From Rupp's History of Berks and Lebanon Counties.*)

The interest which our hero took in the evangelizing of the Indians will become all the more striking when we recall the fact that he spent three months in instructing *Pyrlacus, Buettner* and *Zander* — missionaries from Europe in 1741 — in the Maqua or Mohawk language at Tulpehocken, during 1743, in order to preach the Gospel to the Iroquois, or Six Nations.

The year 1743 was a; busy year for him. The Governor (Thomas) sends him to Shamokin. Of this trip he says: "On the 30th of January, 1743, in the evening, I received the Governor's order, together with the deposition of Thomas McKee, and set out next morning with Mr. McKee for Shamokin, where we arrived on the 1st of February. I left Shamokin the 6th and arrived at home in the night, the 9th of February."

In April the interests of Virginia and Maryhmd require his services. The Governor of Pennsylvania, accordingly, sends him to the same place. His own words are these: "In April, 1743, I arrived at Shamokin (9th), by order of the Governor of Pennsylvania, to accpiaint the neighboring Indians, and those of Wyoming, that the Governor of Virginia was well pleased with the mediation, and was willing to come to agreement with the Six Nations about the land his people were settled upon, if it was *that* they

36

contended for, and to make up the matter of the late unhappy skirmish in an amicable way."

But he is not permitted to recruit long in his Tulpehocken home. It was the opinion of the Board that Conrad Weiser should be immediately sent for and despatched to Onondago again. Instructions, given under the hand and lesser seal of the Province of Pennsylvania, dated June 18, 1743, were put into his possession. He was charged with delivering the good will of the Governor and Council of Virginia, with the distribution of £100; and with authority to arrange the time and place of meeting during the coming spring, in order to form a Treaty in regard to some disputed lands. Here are five hundred more miles to be gone over. By the 1st day of August he hands up his Report to the Governor. He kept a Journal, noting nil his experience, "for his memory's sake and satisfaction." We will relate some cullings, since there are "several things mentioned which are mere ceremonies and trifling details."

He went on horseback. He smoked many pipes [1] of Philadelphia tobacco, and told them that "it was enough to kill a man to come such a long and bad road, over hills, rocks, old trees, rivers, to fight through a cloud of vermin, and all kinds of poisonous worms and creeping things, besides being loaded with a disagreeable message." The tawny people laughed at him. He met *Aquoyiota,* an old acquaintance of his, a Chief seventy years old. While there, they feasted him on "hominy, venison, dried eels, squashes and Indian corn-bread."

The Record of Conrad Weiser, covering eleven years of constant service, was above all taint or suspicion. His private life, his official history and his religious zeal all combine to present him a very beautiful character before us. It is a pleasure to hear the good reports, coming in from all sides, which endorse the traditional estimation of the man.

[1] The Pipe of Peace is the Indian Flag of Truce. It is often termed the "Calumet" — for what reason we know not. It consists of a reed some four feet long, inserted in a bowl of red marble, curiously painted over with hieroglyphics and adorned with feathers. Every Nation has its own peculiar decorations.

Chapter Fourteen - Ten More Years of Indian Intercourse, Missions and Duties - 1744-1754

Scenes of blood were frequent in those days. Through Conrad Weiser's philanthropic and wise policy many gory outbreaks were prevented, as our ancestors believed and assured us. But withal they did occur. In April, 1744, Governor Thomas was informed that John Armstrong, an Indian trader, with his two servants, Woodward Arnohl and James Smith, had been murdered at Juniata by three Delawares. Conrad was despatched to the Chiefs, at Shamokin, to look up and demand satisfaction for the deed. The culprits were imprisoned at Lancaster and hanged at Philadelphia. In reference to this matter he says, in a letter, dated Tulpehocken, April 26, 1744: "I am always willing to comply with His honor's commands, but could wish they might have been delayed till after Court, where my presence by many is required on some particular accounts. But as the command is pressing and cannot be delayed, I am prepared to set out to-morrow morning for Shamokin. I mil use the best of my endeavors to have the Governor's and Council's request answered to satisfaction, by delivering up the two Indians and the goods. * * * I am afraid they have made their escape far enough by this time." In May he makes his interesting report. The Delaware Indians acknowledged the deed without pleading "insanity." "It is true," said a Chief, "we, by the instigation of the evil spirit, have murdered." * * * "We have transgressed, and we are ashamed to look up. We have taken the murderer and delivered him up to the relatives of the deceased, to be dealt with according to his works. The dead bodies are buried. Your demand for the goods is very just. We have gotten some, and will do the utmost of what we can to find them all. Our hearts are in mourning, and we are in a dismal condition and cannot say anything at present." A grand feast was prepared for over one hundred persons, who devoured a big, fat bear in silence. A Chief, the oldest, arose and said: "Although, by a great misfortune, three of their white brothers had been murdered by the Indians, the sun had still not gone down, and war set in; but that only a little cloud had crossed the face, which now too had been cleared away; and that all the evil-doers should be punished, whilst the country remained in peace, and the Great Spirit must be praised." He then struck on a musical tune, which all chimed along. No words seemed to be employed — merely a tune, which was very solemnly uttered. At the end the veteran exclaimed: "Thanks! Thanks! To Thee, Great Governor of the World, that Thou hast chased away the clouds and suffered the sun to shine on once more. The Indians are Thy children."

The Great Council was held at Lancaster, Pa., June 22, and a Treaty was made with the Six Nations. The Governor was present, and the Commissioners of Virginia and Maryland. This Conference was a protracted one and ended about the close of July. Many pleasant occurrences are noted as having transpired during the proceedings. The Indians frequently shouted their *"Johah,"* which denotes approbation and good feeling. It is a loud cry, and consists of a few notes pronounced in unison, in a musical manner, in the nature of our 'Hurrah.' Three hundred pounds were distributed among the Indians in presents, of vermilion, flints, jewsharps, boxes, lead, shot, gun-powder, shirts, blankets and guns. Conrad Weiser interpreted, and explained the present. A deed was executed, by which all their claim and title to certain lands lying in the Provinces of Virginia and Marykmd were released. They demanded that Conrad Weiser sliould sign the instrument, as well with his Indian name as with his English. His Indian name was *Tarachawagon.*

The messenger of the Governor of Virginia made the following complimentary allusion to the Interpreter in his address to the Sachems and Warriors of the Six Nations:

"Our friend, Conrad Weiser, when he is old, will go into the other world, as our fathers have done. Our children will then want such a friend, to go between them and your children, to reconcile any differences that may arise between them; who, like him, may have the ears and tongues of our children and yours.

"The way to have such a friend is for you to send three or four of your boys to Virginia, where we have a fine house for them to live in, and a man on purpose to teach children of yours, our friends, the religion, language and customs of the white people. To this place we kindly invite you to send of your children; and we promise you they shall have the same care taken of them, aud be instructed in the same manner as our own children; and be returned to you again when you please. And to confirm this, we give you this string of Wampum."

To this proposition Canassatego replied in these words:

"Brother Assaraquoa: You told us, likewise, you had a great house provided for the education of youths; that there were several white people and Indian children there to learn languages, to read and write; and invited us to send some of our children among you.

"We must let you know we love our children too well to send them so great a way. And the Indians are not inclined to give their children learning. We allow it to be good, and we thank you for your invitation. But our customs differing from yours, you will be so good as to excuse us.

"We hope Tarachawagon (Conrad Weiser) will be preserved by the Great Spirit to a good old age. When he is gone under ground, it will be time enough to look out for another. And, no doubt, amongst so many thousands as there are in the world, one such man may be found who will serve both parties with the same fidelity as Tarachawagon does. While he lives there is no room to complain."

Surely the old Chief had knowledge of a very good sort of philosophy. It was teaching the popular proverb: "Never cross a bridge till you come to it"; or the Christian theory, "Fear not, but trust to Providence."

This apt reply reminds us of another, similar in kind. General George Washington, while President of the United States, sent an Agent to the Chypewyan Tribe, whose friendship it was requisite we should cultivate to preserve the lucrative fur trade. Among other things that the illustrious President offered was, "that the United States would take two or three of the sons of their Chiefs and educate them in our colleges." When the proposition had been offered, the Indians, who never give an immediate answer to things that they think of importance, told the Agent: "They would think of it." After a short time they returned for an answer: "That they had consulted on the subject, and were of the opinion that it would render them effeminate to be educated in our schools, as it would totally disqualify them to hunt or pursue the war; but, in return for the civility of their Chief, Washington, they would, if he would send the sons of his men among them, educate them to pursue the chase for several days without eating; and to go without clothing in extremely cold weather, and, in frosty nights, to lay on the ground without covering, and every other thing requisite to make them Indians and brave men."

The Lancaster Treaty brought Conrad Weiser £15, 3s., 6d., to defray his expenses by.

During this year the Governor sent forth intimations of a war in prospect against the French. In order to keep the Indians on good terms with the English, Conrad Weiser was kept in constant employment. Hearing of the death of a Chief among the Onoudagos, he suggests a visit of condolence, which he was accordingly ordered to perform, in September.

This being a very critical time, the traffic in liquor which the traders carried on for pelf's sake, gave the Government much to do. Reduced to a state of intoxication, they would barter their skins away for a mere song, and after having recovered from a drunken fit, they were ready to seek revenge. Conrad Weiser was the pacificator of the day. Governor Thomas said, at Philadelphia, August 24, 1744: "Tho' the Indian traders are not the best sort of people, and may not do you well, yet you are not to take revenge yourselves, but apply, in all cases, to Conrad Weiser, who is a Justice of the Peace, and will hear your complaints and procure you such redress as our law will give you." The Delawares were satisfied with this advice.

With the opening of 1745 came further duties and tasks for our diligent man. In flanuary, at his suggestion again, he builds a house for Shekallamy, at Shamokiu, "49½ feet long and 17½ wide, and covered with shingles, in 17 days" — which we may regard a speedy job for that period. During this year, too, he gave his eldest daughter in marriage to the grand old Lutheran Patriarch, the Rev. Dr. Henry Melchior Muhlenberg, as we shall learn in another place. But he has little time to spend in festivities at home. French machinations call him, in company with Shekallamy and others, to Onondago again. He sets out on the 19th of May. The result of his negotiations, which opened on the 6th of June, may be seen in a letter of his, to which the reader is referred.

Here we will insert an anecdote, which we extract from Rupp's History of Berks and Lebanon Counties:

"It was probably while at Onondago this time, the current anecdote, related by Dr. Franklin, touching Weiser and Canassatego, which is found in Drake's Indian Biography, Book V., p. 12, 13, originated. As the editors of the valuable Encyclopedia Perthensis have thought this anecdote worthy a place in that work, it has gained one here:

"Dr. Franklin tells us a very interesting story of Canassatego, and at the same time makes the old Chief tell another. In speaking of the manners and customs of the Indians, the doctor says: The same hospitality, esteemed among them as a principal virtue, is practised by private persons; of which Conrad Weiser, our interpreter, gave me the following instances: He had been naturalized among the Six Nations, and spoke well the Mohawk language. In going through the Indian country, to carry a message from our Governor to the Council at Onondago, he called at the habitation of Canassatego, an old acquaintance, who embraced him, spread furs for him to sit on, placed before him some boiled beans, and venison, and mixed some rum and water for his drink. When he was well refreshed, and had lit his pipe, Canassatego began to converse with him; asked how he had fared the many years since they had seen each other; whence he then came; what occasioned the journey, etc. Conrad answered all his questions; and when the discourse began to flag, the Indian, to continue it, said, 'Conrad, you have lived long among the white people, and know something of their customs: I have been sometimes at Albany, and have observed that once in seven days they shut up their shops and assemble in the great house; tell me what that is for; what do they do there "They meet there," says Conrad, "to hear and learn good things." 'I do not doubt,' says the Indian, 'that they tell you so; they have told me the same; but I doubt the truth of what they say, and I will tell you my reasons. I went lately to Albany, to sell my skins, and buy blankets, knives, powder, rum, etc. You know I used generally to deal with Hans Hanson; but I was a little inclined this time to try other merchants. However, I called first upon Hans, and asked him what he would give for beaver. He said he could not give more than four shillings a pound; but, says he, I cannot talk on business now; this is the day when we meet together to learn good things, and I am going to the meeting. So I thought to myself, since I cannot do any business to-day, I may as well go to the meeting too, and I went with him. There stood up a man in black, and began to talk to the people very angrily; I did not understand what he said, but perceiving that he looked much at me, and at Hanson, I imagined that he was angry at seeing me there; so I went out, sat down near the house, struck fire, and lit my pipe, waiting till the meeting should break up. I thought, too, that the man had mentioned something of beaver, and suspected it might be the subject of their meeting. So when they came out, I accosted my merchant. 'Well, Hans,' says I, 'I hope you have agreed to give more than 4s. a pound.' 'No,' says he, 'I cannot give so much; I cannot give more than three shillings and sixpence.' I then spoke to several other dealers, but they all sung the same song, — three and sixpence, three and sixpence. This made it clear to me that my suspicion was right; and that whatever they pretended of meeting to learn good things, the purpose was to consult how to cheat Indians in the price of beaver. Consider but a little, Conrad, and you must be of my opinion. If they met so often to learn good things, they would certainly have learned some before this time. But they are still ignorant. You know our practice. If a white man, traveling through our country, enters one of our cabins, we all treat him as I do you; we dry him if he is wet; we warm him if he is cold, and give him meat and drink, that he may allay his thirst and hunger; and we spread soft furs for him to rest and sleep on: we demand nothing in return. But if I go into a white man's house at Albany, and ask for victuals and drink, they say, 'Get out, you Indian dog.' You see they have not yet learned those little good things, that we need no meetings to be instructed in, because our mothers taught them to us when we were children; and therefore it is impossible their meetings should be, as they say, for any such purpose, or have any such effect: they are only to contrive the cheating of Indians in the price of beaver.'"

In October he is in New York, surrounded by Chiefs. In December he is directed by the Governor, at the suggestion of the Council, to employ scouts among the Shamokin Indians "to watch the enemy's movements, and to engage the whole body of Indians there to harass them in their march. The pay or reward to be given them, in all such transactions, to be entrusted to his own good judgment to determine."

A slight intermission of missionary travel seems to have been granted him during the year 1746. But it was by no means an idle year. As farmer, Justice of the Peace and Interpreter, he found enough to do. It would prove a difficult task to find a character whose record presents a less broken chain.

In 1747 the Proprietary Governor, John Penn, dies. He is charged in June to carry the sad news to the Indians at Shamokin. In October he writes to Secretary Peters and advices that a handsome present should be made to the Indians on the Ohio and Lake Erie * * * "since they, by their situation, were capable of doing much mischief if they should turn to the French."

And in November he is found again at Shamokin. This time Shekallamy, his old friend and friend of the Province, is in the deep waters of affection. Conrad Weiser's heart was not the one that could pass by on the other side, or even but come and look upon him. "I arrived," says he, "at

Shamokin on the 9th, about noon. I was surprised to see Shekallamy in such a condition as my eyes beheld. He was hardly able to stretcli forth his hand to bid me welcome. In the same condition was his wife — his three sons not quite so bad, but very poorly; also one of his daughters and two or three of his grandchildren. All had the fever. There were three buried out of the family a few days before, namely: Cajadis, Shekallamy's son-in-law, who had been married to his daughter above fifteen years, and was reckoned the best hunter among all the Indians, and two others. I administered medicine to them, under the direction of Dr. Graeme. Shekallamy soon recovered from his sickness. The medicine had a very good effect. * * * Four persons thought themselves as good as recovered; but, above all, Shekallamy was able to go about with me, by a stick, before I left Shamokin, which was on the 12th, in the afternoon."

"I must, in conclusion," he goes on to say, "recommend, as an object of charity, Shekallamy. He is extremely poor. In his sickness the horses have eaten all the corn. His clothes he gave to the Indian doctors to cure him and his family; but all did no good. He has nobody to hunt for him, and I cannot see how the poor old man can live. He has been a true servant to the Government, and may still be, if he lives to get well again. As the winter is coming on, I think it would not be amiss to send him a few blankets, or match-coats, and a little powder and lead. If the Government would be pleased to do it, I would send my sons with it to Shamokin, before the cold weather comes." This is the parable of the 'Good Samaritan' in a practical way. He had from his thorough acquaintance with the Gospel, as Muhlenberg says, learned the full import of the admonition of St. James, and failed not to realize it on this poor Indian.

His prayer for charity was not unheeded, either. £16 were given him, which his sons promptly delivered to the unfortunate family.

He informed Secretary Peters that the present, intended for the Ohio Indians, had been dealt out with too sparing a hand. The Council regretted that it had already been forwarded, as it was, but assured him that no further action would be taken in this direction without consultinof him; and requested him to attend the Council at Philadelphia, in view of a conference with the Ohio Warriors.

In November he speaks of his timely arrival at Paxton, to prevent the Indians about there from going over to the French.

His temperance principles came to the surface again and again. He does not look with favor on the liquor traffic with the Indians. "It is an abomination before God and man," as he puts it.

About the close of 1747 and beginning of 1748 a mission to Ohio was spoken of. The Provinces of Virginia and Maryland were asked to join with Pennsylvania in preparing a suitable bribe for the Indians dwelling on the banks of the Ohio river, who were allied to the Six Nations. This

Province alone gathered about ten thousand pounds for this and similar purposes. Conrad Weiser was immediately thought of as the envoy. He endeavored to excuse himself from performing so long and hazardous a journey. But he was finally prevailed on to undertake it, through the earnest words of Secretary Peters. The enterprise was postponed, however, until the 11th day of August, 1748, when he set out from his home at Tulpehocken. We have not the space to remark on all the thrilling incidents, but ninst refer the reader to his Journal. By the second day of October he arrives safe at his home.

In the month of April, 1749, his commission as Justice of the Peace was renewed. By the first day of July he is in Philadelphia, interpreting for the Indians of various tribes. In August Governor Hamilton speaks thus to the Board:

"Mr. Weiser having defrayed the expenses of the last Indians, in their journey to and from this city, I advanced him the sum of £60 on his going way. He must, by this time, have laid out a considerable sum more, which you will please to order payment of. And tho' from your long knowledge of his merits, it might be unnecessary in me to say anything in his favor, yet as the last set of Indians did damage to his plantation, and he had abundant trouble with them and is likely to meet much more on this occasion, I cannot excuse myself from most heartily recommending it to your mind, to make him a handsome reward for his services."

He continued busy with his tawny friends during the entire month, mediating, negotiating, pacifying and laboring in the service.

In this year he, with Secretary Peters, aided by the magistrates of the county, the delegates of the Six Nations, one Chief of the Mohawks, and Andrew Montour, the Interpreter from Ohio, whom Weiser had recommended to the Board as a person of capacity, because of his long residence among the Iroquois, was directed to proceed to Cumberland county, to drive forth certain white squatters and intruders on Indian ground. We, accordingly, find him a member of the Board of Conference, at that place, on the 17th of May, 1750. The balance of the month and a part of Jnly, again, is consumed with some Conestogoe Indians and the Twightccs. Indecil it were, perhaps, more proper to note his rare visits home than his goings abroad, since he seems to be forever roaming at large, whilst his arrivals at home are more like angels' visits. He is the Indian Agent, in fact, during these years. The President of the Province of Virginia, Honorable Thomas Lee, requests him to proceed to Onondago, in August, as usual, on Indian affairs. After an absence of two mouths he returns, "in perfect health, on the first day of October." During this trip he visited his relatives and friends in the Province of New York, his earlier home, and recommends the nephew, Jolm Picket, to the Mohawks as his successor, who resided about one mile from Canawadagy.

In May, 1751, the Governor designed sending him on a second mission to Ohio. He answers, from Tulpehocken, that his presence is more necessary, during the approaching Fall, at Albany, and suggests that substitutes be sent, which request was granted him. In June, however, we find him already at Albany on official business, and in August at Philadelphia again, talking Indian and English, as usual.

In June, 1752, when Moravian missionaries designed to operate on the Six Nations and request suitable passports, Conrad Weiser is first consulhed in the matter, a circumstance which shows still more plainly how perfectly the whole Indian territory, and all matters related thereto, lay under his hand.

Governor Dinwiddie was fearing the presages of thr coming storm in 1753, and requests his jircsence at Albany in behalf of Virginia. He must needs go to the Mohawk country, too. He set out from his home in Heidelberg, July 24th; arrives at New York by the first day of August — "being taken ill, I sent my son Sammy with one Henry Van der Ham to Flushing, on Long Island, to wait on Governor Clinton to deliver Governor Tamilton's letters. August 7th, took passage on board a sloop to Albany." By the close of August he returns to Philadelphia. At Carlisle a part of September is spent with Chiefs of the Six Nations and other tribes. Conrad Weiser and his Indian friends seemed to be flitting about, here, there and everywhere.

But the spare days at home were devoted no less zealously to improvements. He subscribes to a petition for a highway from Reading to Easton. And, as if the man had not a sufficient number of burdens on his shoulders, a company of benevolent men of London, forming a scheme for the instruction of German youths, constituted a General Board of Trustees for its execution, in which the following list of names was made to stand:

Governor James Hamilton, Chief Justice Allen, Richard Peters, Secretary of the Province, Benjamin Franklin, Esq., Conrad Weiser and Rev. William Smith, D. D. The Reverend Michael Schlatter was constituted Visitor General by the Board.

The wonder is that the man did not succumb under the heavy load before this date. We merely sketched his shiftings, from one to several hundred miles distant, his trials, duties and labors. But the mere recital is already fearful. Hardly any one of his cotemporaries held out so long, even under less pressure. Men of his own race retire and die. The hardy Indian, indeed, bends his back and bows his head. Still he clings to life and duty.

Chapter Fifteen - The French and Indian War. Conrad Weiser, Superintendent of the Indian Bureau. Colonel. His Death Officially Announced. 1754-1760

King William's (1689-1697), Queen Anne's (1702-1713) and King George's wars (1744-1748) were followed by the French and Indian war, which extended its bloody trail from 1754 to 1763. The course of the last season of carnage was, the region west of the Allegheny mountains, along the Ohio river. The French territory Kent around from Quebec to New Orleans. The English occupied a narrow strip along the coast one thousand miles in length.

"As unto the bow the cord is," so these tracts were the one to the other. Both parties claimed the disputed ground, regardless of the Indians, who were the real proprietors after all. The French encroached on English parts by breaking up old forts long established and planting new ones. Early in the Spring they became still more aggressive at Port Du Quesne (Pittsburg), which was the key to the region west of the Alleghenies. As long as this point was held by them, Virginia and Pemisylvania were a battlefield. The Colonies spent $16,000,000 in this war, and suffered such horrid Indian cruelties as never were and never will be told.

Washington and Braddock were the principal figures on the field; Benjamin Franklin was the central head in the Provincial Cabinet, and Conrad Weiser was Superintendent of the Indian Department. In April, 1754, the Governor sent Conrad Weiser to Shamokin on a mission of inquiry and conciliation among the Chiefs over some of the Six Nations. In June he accompanies Benjamin Franklin to Albany. These are some of Governor Hamilton's words: "I have, agreeably to your desire, sent Mr. Weiser, with the Commissioners, and directed him to do you all the service in his power, which he professes most willingly to do; and only recpiests that he may not be made use of as a principal Interpreter, inasmuch as from a disuse of the language he is no longer master of that fluency he formerly had, and, finding himself at a loss of proper terms to express himself, is frequently obliged to make use of circumlocution, which would pique his pride in the view of so considerable an audience. He says he understands the language perfectly when he hears it spoken, and will at all times attend and use his endeavor that whatever is said by the Indians be truly interpreted to the gentlemen. And in this respect I really think you may securely rely on his good sense and integrity."

This Council at Albany, lasting through June, July and part of August, was a very important one. Here the first "Plan of Union" for the Colonies was suggested; more lands were purchased from the Indians and Deeds executed, to which instruments the names of Franklin, Weiser and others were subscribed.

In August he is sent to Aucquick, to learn the mind and relations of the Indian dwellers there. In December he aids the Governor in framing suitable messages to the Tribes.

In the beginning of 1755 (January) he is sent for "by express" to come to Philadelphia. Let it be borne in mind that "by express" did not mean a swift and easygoing air passage, but, at best, on horseback — which again meant to go on foot by more than half the distance, leading the horse by the bridle. The Mohawks had brought news touching the Connecticut people, and Conrad Weiser was needed to talk it over. In June we find him to have been engaged in providing for his Indian friends, some forty-five miles above Shamokin, on the northwest branch of the Susquehanna. John Harris demands his presence, likewise, at this time on account of savage depradations. So too, in July following, whilst acting in the capacity of a quarter-master for some needy Indians, the presence of the Owendotts at Philadelphia called him "by express" thither.

One would think that when the country luul been in such a state of unrest, no one would be likely to dream of a religious conspiracy. Still, noless than five Justices of Berks county subscribed to a prayer, addressed to the Council, asking that a certain Catholic Chapel at Goshenhoppen be looked after, since there were rumors of Indians occupying it with arms. After some little inquiry it was found that there seemed to be but little foundation to such a rumor.

During this period, when sent for to come to Philadelphia in haste, he reports himself as indisposed. This is the second time that he complains of being unwell. He sends his son, Samuel, as a substitute, who had previously accompanied him on some of his expeditions. In August he is promptly at his post again, attending no less than three different conferences. In September Governor Morris sends him to Harris' Ferry. The month of October he spends at home, though his sons, Frederick and Peter, had to go to Shaniokin in his stead. His household seems to have been in the employ of the Province, as well as he.

On the 31st day of October Governor Morris forwards his commission as "Colonel." He accompanies the letter with some complimentary words: "I heartily commend your conduct and zeal, and hope you will continue to act with the same vigor and caution that you have already done, and that you may have a greater authority, I have appointed you a Colonel by a commission herewith. I have not time to give you any instructions with the commission, but leave it to your judgment and discretion, which I know are great, to do what is most for the safety of the people aud service of the crown." Was this not a Carte-Blanche?

No one will imagine Conrad Weiser to have proven a mere ornamental Colonel, verily. He commanded a regiment of volunteers from the county of Berks, and had command over the Second Battalion of the Pennsylvania regiment, consisting of nine companies. "He exerted himself by day and night, in the protection of his suffering neighbors and fellow-citizens, and repelling the savage Indians in their incursions. He was vigilant, brave and active, in the full sense of the terms. A number of forts and block houses were erected under his directions on the frontiers of Lancaster and Berks. * * * He distributed his companies very judiciously — stationing one company at Fort Augusta, one at Hunter's Mills, seven miles above Harrisburg, on the Susquehanna; one-half company on the Swatara, at the foot of the North Mountain; one company and a half at Fort Henry, close to the gap of the mountain, called the *Tolhea Gap;* one company at Fort William, near the forks of the Schuylkill river, six miles beyond the mountain; one company at Fort Allen, erected by Benjamin Franklin, at Gnadenhuetten, on the Lehigh; the other three companies were scattered between the rivers Lehigh and Delaware, at the dispositions of the ctains, some at farm houses, others at mills, from three to twenty at a place." — *Rupp.*

But though a Colonel in active service, he dare not absent himself from the many Conferences and Treaty-makings which were being held at short intervals during these years. In November, 1755, he is in Philadelphia, with two hard cases on his hands — Scarrozady and drunken Tigrea. Here is a specimen of a speech:

"We tell you the French have a numerous alliance of other Indians, as well as the Delawares, in this war."

(Danced the war dance.)

"When Washington was defeated, we, the Delawares, were blamed as the cause of it. We will now kill. We will not be blamed without a cause. We make up three parties of Delawares. One party will go against Carlisle, one down the Susquehanna, and I myself, with another party, will go against Tulpehocken, to Conrad Weiser."

The revolted Delawares caused much anxiety to the Government, and Conrad Weiser was the only man who could effect anything with them. In December his letters and reports were forwarded, and thus another year came to its close.

Harris' Ferry claims his services during .January of 1756. He accompanies Governor Morris and James Logan to Carlisle, during the same month, where a Conference was held. Back again to Harris' Ferry and Philadelphia in February. A good part of July is spent at Easton. Certain insinuations in Christian Sowers' paper, at Germantown, to the effect that the ill-will of the Indians had been excited by the dishonest and covetous spirit of the Government, offends his honor, in September, for which he reports the editor and wants him punished. It turned out not quite as bad as he had thought, however, and he and Sowers were fast friends to the end of his life.

In October Shayetowah, John Shekallamy's brother, complains of having lost his friend Conrad Weiser, before the Board, and expresses a strong inclination to see him again. He might have seen him on this occasion, but, alas! the old Interpreter is unwell for the third time. He could not travel, though asked to come "by express." Long exposure and age are beginning to tell, for he is now in his sixtieth year. His son, Samuel, is his proxy again, who, by the way, is styled "Captain Sam." But in November he had recruited, and goes to Easton.

The Indians desire a Council to be held there, and Conrad Weiser so arranged it. The Governor did not fancy to go abroad, and thought it unnecessary to gratify such whims of theirs. But Conrad knew better, and the proposed Council was held, which proved an important one, lasting nearly three weeks.

During this year he took up his residence in Reading, at the corner of Penn and Callowhill streets. In old times it was the principal hotel in the place. "Here," says the *Reading Times,* "the war song of the savage was sung, the war dance wound down and the calumet of peace finally smoked." The house was built in 1751 and known as the "Wigwam." Many a Conference was held within its walls, and Treaties effected under its roof, in the old Indian Agent's day. The walls are still standing np to the second story.

In 1757 he, with Logan, prepared the Governor's message to the Six Nations. In May he does the same service for a Council Member, Crogham, who undertook the task of replying to the Delaware Indians, but failed.

The condition of the frontier settlers was truly deplorable at this period. Sickness and savages made their lot a hard one, indeed. Appeals to the Government were made, but a deaf ear was turned to their cries. The following appeal we copy from Rupp's History of Berks and Lebanon Counties:

"Die hintern Einwohner zu Dopehocken bitten um eine Beysteuer, dasz sie mehr Waeten bezahlen kennen zu ihrer Sicherheit, weil die Festungen so weit anseinander liegen und die Voelcker drinnen wenig Dienste thunn. Wer willen ist, etwas zu steuern, der kann es ablegen in Lancaster bei Herrn Oterbein, und Herrn Gerock, Luth. Pred.; in New Hanover und Providentz by Mr. Muehlenberg und Leydig; in Madetsche by Dr. Abrahain Wagner; in Goschenhoppen by Mr. Michael Reyer; in Germantown by Christoph Sauer, Sr., und in Philadelphia bey Hr. Hundshuh, und dabey schreiben, wie viel gegeben worden; und diese koennen es uebersenden an Col. Conrad Weiser; oder Peter Spycher, oder an Hr. Kurtz, wie es einem Jeden beliebt.

"Diejenigen, welche in Ruhe und Sicherheit ihre Erndte haben koennen schneiden und heimbringen, haben Ursache, Gott davor zu danken."

That Conrad Weiser could not please every Indian may be seen from the following remarks of Tecdyuscuug, Delawarian Chief, uttered in the month of July:

"I was deceived by Conrad Weiser, who promised to give me notice (to call on the Governor), but he broke his word with me. And if he could do it in this instance, he may do it in another."

The Governor plead a misunderstanding, and begged the Chief to suspend judgment till an explanation could be had. This occurred at Easton, where a protracted Council was held, and resulted in a Treaty. At a meeting of the Board, September 12th, Mr. Weiser was ordered to build a house for the Delaware Indians at Wyoming. The bloody-minded Teedyuscung was inclined to have a price fixed for scalps. By request Conrad Weiser uttered his mind on the subject in these words: "It is my humble opinion that no encouragement should be given to the Indians for scalps, for fear we must then pay for our own scalps, and those of our fellow subjects, as will certainly be the case. Allow as much for prisoners as you please — rather more than was intended." He ever remained a humane man, though among the savages for a lifetime.

As to building a house at Wyoming, he seemed to be in doubt. At all events, he was unwilling to attend to it. "I am in a very low state of health, and cannot, without great hazard, undertake any journey."

Previous to this writing we find him, during 1757, at a Treaty-making in Lancaster, in May, and also again in Easton, in August. His rare appearance, during the last two years, is explained by the part of the letter just quoted. It seems odd to the eye, that has accustomed itself to find his name on so many successful pages, now to find strange names, now of this man, then of that one, in his familiar room. But all things end.

In 1760 the Indian Agents at Fort Augusta inform the Council that John Shekallamy is anxious to see Conrad Weiser. The Secretary had written to him and asked him to take the trouble upon himself to go to Shamokin. The answer was that he could not go, but that he wcjuld send his son Samuel. And lo! his name appears never again as Interpreter.

There is a record, though, which we extract from the minutes of an Indian Conference held at Easton, and insert, as in good place, here. It bears the date August 3d, 1761, and reads thus:

"Seneca George stood up and spoke as follows:

"Brother Onas: We, the Seven Nations, and our cousins are at a great loss and sit in darkness, as well as you, by the death of Conrad Weiser, as since his death we cannot so well understand one another. By this belt we cover his body with bark.

"Brother Onas: Having taken notice of the death of Conrad Weiser, and the darkness it has occasioned amongst us, I now by this belt raise up another Interpreter, by whose assistance we may understand one another clearlv. You know that in former times, when men grew old and died, we used to put others in their places. Now, as Conrad Weiser (who was a great man, and one-half a Seven Nation Indian and one-half an Englishman) is dead, we recommend it to the Governor to appoint his son (pointing to Samuel, then present) to succeed him as an Interpreter, and to take care of the Seven Nations and their cousins."

The Governor, James Hamilton, answered: "Brethren: We are very sensible, with you, that both of us have sustained a very heavy loss by the death of our old and good friend, Conrad Weiser, who was an able, experienced and faithful Interpreter, and one of the Council of the Seven Nations; mid that since his death we, as well as you, have sat in darkness, and are at a great loss for want of well understanding what we say to one another. We mourn with you for his death, and heartily join in covering his body with bark.

"Brethren: Having thus paid our regards to our deceased friend, we cannot but observe with you that there is a necessity of appointing some other person to succeed him, by whose assistance we may be enabled to find the true sense and meaning of what there may be occasion to say to one another, either in Council, or by letters or messages.

"Brethren: In conformity to the ancient custom of taking from among the relations of any man who dies, some fit person to supply his place (as Mr. Weiser was by adoption one of the Six Nations, though by birth one of us), we think you did well to cast your eyes upon one of his children; and, inasmuch as Samuel Weiser is the only one amongst them who has any knowledge of the Indian language, and has lived among you, we shall be glad to make trial of him for the present, and if we find him capable of serving in the office of Interpreter and in the management of Indian affairs (in both which capacities his father so well acquitted himself), we shall appoint him to that service. We look upon this choice of yours as a mark of your grateful aifection for Conrad Weiser, who was always your sincere friend, and we join this belt to yours in token of our concurrence as far as to make trial of him."

In a letter of Secretary Peters, dated Feb. 12, 1761, Philadelphia, we read: "Poor Mr. Weiser is no more; he died suddenly in the summer, and has not left any one to fill his place as Provincial Interpreter. His son, Samuel, has almost forgotten what little he knew."

Thus closes his Indian record. From 1724 to the end of his life he had been among, and in almost daily intercourse with the Indians, a period extending over forty-six years.

If Thomas Jefferson felt prompted to say of Lewis and Clarke and their brave companions that they "deserved well of their country," who (from 1804-6) performed a journey of 3,000 miles, through an unexplored portion of the Continent, covered with Indian Tribes, we need not hesitate to affirm the same of Conrad Weiser, who did a greater thing, and in a still more difficult era of the country's history. In imitation of Charles Tiamb we say:

"When mortals, such as he was, die,
  Their place we may not well supply,
  Though we among a thousand try.
  With vain endeavor."

Chapter Sixteen - Conrad Weiser's Failing Health. His Death. His Burial-Place

During the last five years of his busy and trying life Conrad Weiser showed signs of a wearing down and coming dissolution. On several occasions he could not respond to the call of the Government, as we have seen, because of indisposition. When he was appointed Colonel in 1755, he was infirm — too much so to discharge the onerous duties of the office, one may say. His son-in-law says: "*Er war schon alt an Jahren, schwach an Leibeskraeften, etc.*" And yet, though verging on sixty, he seemed to perform with vigor and promptness all the functions of Interpreter, Justice and Soldier. He had lived too long and well to succumb at once. Men may not die when they will, nor always when they might. The sad privilege of shortening one's life implies the prerogative of lengthening it, too, in a measure. We may master circumstances to a degree, even though we are mastered by them finally. The state of his health had already indicated an abandonment of public life, when the burdens of a Colonelcy were imposed upon him; but the pressure from without and the patriotic impulse from within did not permit him to give up and retire.

However, all things end in this world, and we speak of the mighty as fallen, sooner or later. On September 19, 1759, he writes: "I am in a very low state of health, and cannot, without great hazard, undertake any journey." On the 24th day of the following November he signs and seals his last will and testament, an act in which man shows that he has learned to know himself a mortal. How plainly the confession is embodied in the adjunct *"last!"*

On the 12th day of July, 1760, eight months later, on a Saturday, as he left his home in Reading, in his average health, he was seized with a violent attack of colic, which ended his life on the following Sunday (13th), about the hour of noon. Thus died Conrad Weiser, July 13, 1760, on his farm at Womelsdorf. On the loth, the Rev. John Nicholas Kurtz, Lutheran Pastor at Tulpehocken, Lebanon county, preached his funeral discourse on the two-fold text in Genesis 15: 15, and Psalm 84: 11-12: "And thou shall go to thy fathers in peace; thou shalt be buried in a good old age." — *"For the Lord God is a sun and shield: the Lord will give grace and glory: no good thing will be withheld from them that walk uprighth. O Lord of hosts, blessed is the man that trusteth in thee."*

Unfortunately Conrad Weiser owned a private burying ground, in which his mortal remains were interred, the spot lies one-half mile east of the town of Womelsdorf, south of the turnpike road. A rough-hewn sandstune, single and alone, stands over his dust. The following epitaph may, with difficulty, be deciphered:

"Dies ist die
Ruhe Staette des
weyl. Ehren geachteten M. Conrad Weiser; derselbige ist gebohren 1696 den 2. November in Alstaet im Amt Harrenberg im Wittenberger Lande, und gestorben
1760 den 13. Julius, ist
alt worden 63 Jahr,
8 Monat und 13 Tag."

Pastor Muhlenberg is probably the framer of this inscription.

It is held as true that ludians frequently visited his tomb, for many years after, out of affectionate regard for their old friend.

I. D. Rupp, Esq., says he "visited the grave of Weiser, February 21, 1844, and was pained to see no enclosure or fence around the grave of so great and good a man." For the letter "M." in his epitaph we cannot account — if it is really an *M.* Our ancestors told us it stood for the German term *Mann,* — *des geachteten Mannes, etc.*

A desolate tomb is a sad spectacle — but only for mortals, who see where they must shortly lie. Blessed are the dead, who heed it not.

Neither do the weight and shadows of great monuments contribute anything towards an immortality. There is no life in a stone, and it can create none. Pillars and shafts have never yet immortalized a dead man, though they do oftentimes entomb him all the more. The 'living dead' die no more, whilst the 'buried dead' are forgotten, even if the stone remain — to tell how dead they are. The Pyramids endure, but who may tell the Pharaohs in and underneath? The dust of Priestly lay long quite unostentatiously at Northumberland; yet his disciples could ever find it. Governor Simon Snyder's ashes are covered by a low prostrate marble, at Selinsgrove, without line or letter of an epitaph, and still his grave is known. Only the 'dwellers in tombs' need imposing sentinels, lest we know not where we tread.

Of what avail, then, are monuments? They ought to be planted as disinterested testimonials to worth and virtue. As proofs of an immortality, rather than as promoters of it, we value them. When they are challenged, more than imposed, are they appropriate only. As marks of the habitation of distinguished dust, they are not a mockery. There is a kinship between the mounds, manes and men, which Pagans, Mohammedans, Jews and Christians feel and acknowledge; and this bond the Hame of cremation, even, may not dissolve.

After a little while and the grave of Conrad Weiser can no longer be known by Indian or white man. Some becoming mark there should be, on which to engrave the almost obliterated inscription:

> *"This is the*
> *resting-place of*
> *the once honored and respected*
> **Conrad Weiser,**
> *who was born November 2d, A. D. 1696,*
> *in Afstaedt, County of Herrenberg, Wurtemberg,*
> *and died July 13th, A. D. 1760,*
> *aged 63 years, 8 months and 13 days."*

A respectable citizen of Womelsdorf writes: "If any man in Berks county deserves a monument, it is Conrad Weiser."

Chapter Seventeen - Conrad Weiser as a Religious Character

Conrad Weiser was a Lutheran *von Haus aus*. His ancestry had been born and reared in this persuasion. He forgets not to tell us of his baptism at Kueppingen. The Reverend Christopher Bockenmeyer, Lutheran minister, baptized a number of his children. But back of that formation, which tradition and education had established in his constitution, lay a sensitive and deep religious temperament, inherited, perhaps, from his excellent mother, which began to manifest itself already in early childhood, became more and more apparent in the period of youth, and remained patent during his long and trying man-age. In his manuscript-record he adopted the habit of crowning every paragraph with apt and pointed Scriptural selections, which betrays the spirit that animated his soul. In his fifteenth year he said: "I became so much attached to my Bible that I looked upon it as my comfort, and it became my book of delight." We feel like denominating him a religious enthusiast, and that of the Pietistic order. The hymns of his composition are of this tenor. Hence it was that his piety carried him again and again beyond his denominational setting. Whether it was because of the fact that his beloved Anna Eva had been of the Reformed Church, or because he was more partial to Pastor Haeger than to Parson Kocherthal, we have it, at all events, over his own hand, that he was given in narrative by the Reformed clergyman at Scoharie.

We know little of significance, touching his religious history, until we find him at Tulpehocken, some six years. In the year 1735 his enthusiasm breaks forth in a noteworthy manner. The advent of Conrad Reiser, a ho^us monk and founder of the German Seventh Day Baptists, marks an epoch in his spiritual life. The unsettled and formal condition of the Germanic Churches in Pennsylvania had doubtless told most sadly on the morals and religion of their membership. An excitement was challenged, produced and fostered. Beisel placed his "candle-stick in the benighted region of Tulpehocken," and with the aid of his sanguine disciples succeeded in creating an awakening. John Peter Miller, a Reformed missionary from the Palatinate, in 1726, officiated as pastor in Tulpehocken at this period. He and his Elders and prominent members, as well as Conrad Weiser and his Lutheran associates, devoted themselves heartily to the work of 'Revival,' and were themselves eddied into and engulfed by it. During May of 1735 Pastor Miller, Conrad Weiser, the Chorister, three Elders of the Tulpehocken Church, and a number of family-heads were initiated into the Association by immersion. This episode is as 'the fly in the ointment,' in the otherwise fair life of the man and hero; and becomes especially objectionable in view of the radicalism with which he pursued his new and pseudo religion, to the injury of his former creed. On a certain day Miller, Weiser and others assembled at the house of Godfried Fidler's, and after having collected the Heidelberg Catechism, Luther's Catechism, the Walter and several other time-honored Books of Devotion, burned them to ashes. Like all perverts from the faith of their forefathers, he showed his love and zeal for his adopted fanaticism, not so much in deeds of charity and proofs of regeneration, as by dishonoring the parental theory and practice by which he came to a knowledge of fundamental truth pertaining to God, and man's relation to Him. There is a genuine conversion possible for man, and such a radical one, too, as involves a very antipodal position to the one previously occupied; but in all cases of genuine revolutions of this kind, a convert will not feel himself obliged to transgress 'the first commandment with promise' by kicking his spiritual mother. Such conduct argues a perversion, rather than a conversion, in every instance. John Philip Boehm, Reformed Pastor, in Whitpain township, Philadelphia county, in his blasts against the Baptists, and efforts of Count Zinzendorf, in 1742, says with much sarcasm of Conrad Weiser: "Der ist, wie die gemeine Sage ist, ein 'Justice.' * * * Und es ist noch nicht bekannt worden, dasz er, seit der Zeit, durch Buse widergekehret und sich widerum zu seiner vorhin gehabten Lutherischen Religion verfueget."

His fall may be somewhat mitigated by the fact, that Pastor Miller, who had been an educated and zealous laborer in the Church and a student from the University of Heidelberg, led the way from home. The shepherd led the sheep astray. But this only for a short season. (See Weiser's letter of withdrawal in Appendix, dated 1743.) Conrad Weiser held out but for a very brief period in his new quarters, as Beisel writes: "He was soon entrapped in the net of his own wisdom." This imitation monk had forebodings, it seems, already from the start, of his coming apostasy, in consequence of some curious pedal examination he had made; had warned him, accordingly, of the peculiar temptation to which he stood exposed, and endeavored to prevent the relapse. "But, in spite of all this caution he fell a victim to the blood-thirsty avenger. Yea, though he had subjected himself to a most vigorous penance, which completely emaciated him, and sutlercd his beard to grow to such a length that no one knew him any longer, and had voluntarily contributed of his possessions for the furtherance of the Society's welfare — still, he fell away."

But, after going so far from home, it is hardly possible to again arrive there in so short a time. The brethren of the homestead will, at all events, not hold them above suspicion. Hence we may term Conrad Weiser a sort of religious vagrant, ever after. His spiritual activity seems to be all circumference without centre. He is all things to all men, without being anything to himself, in a religious sense — perhaps as dangerous a spiritual state as one can well occupy.

In 1738 his ardor and zeal are enlisted in the grand ideal of converting the Indians, in company with Bishop Spangenberger, David Zeisberger and Shebosch, Moravian missionaries. Like a full-built herald of the cross he accompanies them to Onondago. So, too, he becomes a willing yokefellow to Count Zinzendorf, in 1742, on a similar errand to Bethlehem, Shamokin and Philadelphia. He was so full of the Moravian spirit just now that he instructed Pvrlacus, Buettner and Zander in the Mohawk tongue, in order to qualify them to preach the Gospel among the Iroquois. Once he writes of the success of this movement in these words: "I thought myself seated in a company of primitive Christians."

But in 1743 his ardor seems to cool in this direction, too. A Providential man appears on the American territory, who brings the erring man back to the Church of his fathers. The Rev. Henry Melchior Muhlenberg, D. D., who had emigrated in 1742 as the Apostle of Lutheranism in America, visited the Tulpehocken region in 1743. Doubtless both Muhlenberg and Weiser found in each other something of complemental parts. They learned to know and esteem one another at once. Their friendship ripened into a relationship — that of father-in-law and son-in-law. This is very delicately told by the Lutheran Patriarch after this manner: *"Im Jahr 1743 ward unser Freund, Conrad Weiser, bekannt mit dem ersten hereingesandten Deutschen Evangelischen Prediger, gewann ihn und seine Lehre lieb und gab ihm 1745 seine aelteste Tochter zur Ehegenossin. Diese Freundschafts-Verbindung verursachte dann und wann einen Besuch und eine anhaltende Correspondenz; beide wurden, so viel Gott Gnaden verliehen, auf die Seelen-Erbauung gerichtet, wobei er verschiedene Jahre ziemlich munter und lebhaft im Glauben schien. Die heilige Bibel war ihm durch und durch bekannt."*

The influence of his illustrious son-in-law unquestionably did much towards restoring the spiritually wayward man to his proper equilibrium. We hear no more of his religious wandering. But to steady and properly root again one who has so fearfully uprooted himself is no easy matter. We fear Conrad Weiser was never himself again since his Beisel experience. Pastor Muhlenberg's words in reference to the close of his father-in-law's career have an ambiguous ring. Hear and judge:

"Als aber der gefaehrliche Krieg in diesem Theile der Welt zwischen den Franzosen und England ausbrach und unsere benachbarten wilden Nationen meist bundbruechig worden, den Feinden zufielen und unsere Grenzen verwuesteten, gerieth Conrad Weiser in neue Versuchungen. Die Landes Obrigkeit verordnete ihn zum Obrist Leutnant. Die Aemter sind hier bisweilen nur für Personen, und die Personen uicht für die Aemter geschaffen.

"Und weil man seiner nun besonders in diesen Umstaenden benoethigt war und ihm noch viel mehr Mühe und Last auflegen wollte, so sollte das Salarium einst Obrist Leutnauts Alles ersetzen...Diese Bedienung, Charge, oder Last, wie man es nennen mag, that ihm und seinen Kindern mehr Schaden an Seel und Leib, als einiger zuvor. Er war schon alt an Jahren, schwach an Leibeskraeften, der haeuslichen Pflege gewohnt, muszte viel abwesend von Haus sein und auch oft mit den Vornehmen in der Stadt und europaeischen Kriegshelden wegen den Indianer Sachen conferiren.

"Der allergnaedigste und erbarmungsvolle Mittler und Menschenfreund, der nicht Lust hat an des Menschenverderben, erhielt sein natürliches Leben bis fast zuin Ende des wunderlichen Krieges, und verlich ihm noch eine besondere Gnadenfrist, so dasz er Zeit hatte, sich zu recolligiren; im Blute des Lammes die Befleckung des Geistes abzuthun, seine Kleider hell zu machen, seine Seeligkeit mit Furcht und Zittern zu schaffen und ein gnaediges Ende zu erwarten. Es kostet gewisz viel, ein Christ zu sein und zu bleiben."

The weather-vane character of his creed is still further proclaimed by the two items following, which we find entered in the Bible of our late father, to wit:

a) During the razing and rebuilding of the Reformed Church edifice at Reading, Berks county, the name of Conrad Weiser was found on the list of the Building Committee.

b) From a letter of Bishop Spangenberg, dated Toamencin, Montgomery county, Nov. 8, 1737, we gather this extract: "I have made the acquaintance of a certain man, Conrad Weiser, who was nurtured in the faith of the Reformed Church, but who has for some time been identified with the Seventh Day Baptists."

Chapter Eighteen - Conrad Weiser's Will. His Possessions. His Sons and Daughters. His Posterity

Conrad Weiser had been of a prolific ancestry, and was himself the father of fifteen children, eight of which seem to have died in their minority years. His seven surviving ones, made mention of in his last Will and testament, were: Philip, Frederick, Samuel, Benjamin, Peter, Anna Maria and Margaret.

Their father having died, possessed of nearly one thousand acres of land, which were by devise shared out among themselves, the sons naturally took to farming as their principal employment. The manner in which he disposed of his possessions, and to whom, we can best gather from his Will:

"In the name of God. Amen. I, Conrad Weiser, of the town of Reading, in the county of Berks, in the province of Pennsylvania, gentleman, being of perfect health of body and of sound and disposing mind and memory (blessed be God for the same), yet considering the uncertainty of human life and desirous to put myself as far as I may of the cares of this world, do make this my last will and testament, hereby revoking and making void all other and former wills by me heretofore made. *Imprimis.* I do will and order that such debts as may be owing by me at the time of my decease with my funeral expenses be paid by my executors hereafter named as soon as conveniently may be after my decease. *Item.* I give, devise and bequeath unto my beloved wife, Ann Eve, the messuage and lot whereon I now live in the town of Reading, to hold to her, my said wife, during the term of her natural life, and after my said wife's decease I will and order the said messuage and lot to be sold by my executors or the survivor or survivors of them for the best price that can be had for the same, and the money arising from the sale thereof to be divided among all my children or their representatives, share and share alike. *Item.* I give, devise and bequeath unto my said wife Aun(e) and to her heirs forever my lot of ground situate in Callowhill street, in the said town of Reading, marked in the plan of said town, No. 72. *Item.* I give and bequeath unto my said wife an annuity or yearly sum of twenty pounds (interest on) for and during her natural life, or until she marry again, to be paid as hereinafter directed. *Item.* I give and bequeath unto my said wife two of my best feather beds, of her own choice; all my kitchen utensils, and the sum of fifty pounds, current money of Pennsylvania, to be paid to my said wife by my executors within one month after my decease, which I do declare to be in lieu of her dower and full discharge of all demands she may make on my estate. I give, devise and bequeath unto my four sons, Philip, Frederick, Samuel and Benjamin, that is to say to each of my said sons and his heirs for ever, the part of a share to him allotted in a Draft Plan signed with my own proper hand and to this will annexed of all that my plantation in Heidelberg, in the said county of Berks, and my several tracts of land lying contiguous, containing in the whole about eight hundred and ninety acres, — they, my said sons, paying each of thorn the sum of two hundred and fifty pounds lawful money of the said province unto my executors, for the use hereinafter mentioned, within one year after my decease."

Then follow the apportionments and payments, as per plan or draft.

"*Item.* I give and bequeath unto my children, Philip, Frederick, Peter, Samuel, Benjamin, Maria Muhlenberg and Margaret Fiuker, all those my lands lying beyond the Kittochtany mountain, and all my grants or rights to lands lying beyond the same mountains, to be divided in manner following, that is to say (the lands being described) with the Proviso — I do order and direct my executors to secure out of the whole capital the annuity or yearly sum of twenty pounds hereinbefore bequeathed to my said wife in such manner as shall be agreeable to her and correspondent to this my will. And I do will and order that the shares of my children be paid to them respectively within twelve months after my decease, or sooner if the same can conveniently be done. But if my son Benjamin should then be under age, it is my will and order that his brethren put the same to interest, and mortgage it to his best advantage during his minority."

Other provisions follow relative to his grandson, Israel Heintzelman. "*Item.* One hundred pounds out of the share allotted to his mother, which shall be put to interest and managed for his best advantage until he arrives at the age of twenty-one years, and then be paid to him with the profits thereof, and the remaining part of my said daughter Margaret's share of the residuary part of my estate, I do order and direct my executors to put the same to interest on good security and pay her yearly the interest thereof during her natural life. Provided, nevertheless, if my said daughter doth educate her children in the principles and according to the rites of the Roman Church. In such case (or after the death of the said Margaret) it is my will and I do order and direct my executors or the survivors of them, with the consent of my other children as soon as the same is aianifest to them, to retain the interest of money of my said daughter's share and manage the same to the best advantage for the use of her children, to be paid to them in equal shares, together with the principal, as they shall respectively attain the age of twenty-one years. And I do constitute and appoint my wife Ann(e) Eva and my sons Peter and Samuel executors of this my last will and testament. In witness whereof I have hereunto set my hand and seal this twenty-fourth day of November in the year of our Lord one thousand seven hundred and fifty-nine.

Conrad Weiser. [Seal.]
James Whitehead,
Abraham Brossus,
James Biddle."

Subscribing witnesses:

This will was sworn to by James Biddle and Abraham Brossus, July 31, 1760, on which day it was registered in the "General Office, Reading, Berks County."

"Letters testamentary in common form under the seal of the said office on the will above written of the said Conrad Weiser were granted to Ann(e) Eve Weiser, Peter Weiser and Samuel Weiser therein named, they being first solemnly sworn thereto according to law."

Inventory thereof to be exhibited on or before the 31st day of August and an account of their administration when thereunto required.

Registered and examined by James Reed.

The plan or explanation of the draft is appended.

On the corner of Penn and Callowhill streets, Reading, stood Weiser's house, erected in 1751. It was for many years used as a wigwam, where the Indians met for treaty. After his decease it was used as a dwelling-house and partly as a tavern up to 1798, when John Keim and sons commenced business as Iron and Hardware Merchants and was known as "The White Store," which they continued up to 1803; by G. B. D. Leim to 1810; by B. Keim until 1817: by G. B. D. Keim and his son to 1837; by Keim and Stiehter to 1841; by Stichter and McKnight to 1858, when it came into possession of Mr. Joseph L. Stichter.

The deed conveying the property from the executors of Conrad Weiser to Wm. Bird is dated Sept. 30, 1715, and recites the deed granted by the Penns in 1751 to Weiser. The consideration was £554, 5s., subject to a ground rent of 7s. Another conveys the same by Mark Bird and Mary Bird to Nicholas Keim (William having died intestate.) Another, January 16, 1799, to John Keim. Another to G. B. D. Keim. There is also a quit claim deed from the attorney of the Penns to G. B. D. Keim, 1826. Another deed, 1842, from G. B. D. Keim to Joseph L. Stichter and James McKnight for the same property.

From the foregoing instrument it will be known that the sire left a goodly territory of hind to be divided among his children. From the good-will which the Indians invariably cherished for him, as well as from the flattering recommendations which the authorities were ever ready to impress, as an imprimatur, on his oflieial acts, we are warranted to believe that Conrad Weiser came honestly by his thousand acres. Lieut. Governor Thomas says of him, April 25, 1743: "Our Indian Interpreter is a man of *great probity* and a thorough knowledge of Indian affairs." We have the record of a fair negotiation and purchase of a good portion of his possessions, besides, preserved in some of his letters. To Secretary Peters he writes, July 17, 1748: "As Mr. Parsons will (I hope) deliver this to you, with a draft of that piece of land he laid out for me, by your order (I find it is above 400 acres) he will cut off on the side of the hill, if you require it, so much as you shall think fit. But I would rather have it all, and pay to the Honorable proprietors, as they (or you) shall think fit. I don't doubt but what their Honors will let me have it as soon as any other man. Therefore, I pray, let it be conveyed to me and I will do what will be required of me. The other small tract I had surveyed to me by Proprietary Warrant, on the usual conditions; also the right of William Eonst to 37 acres joining. I would have a patent, for a good part is paid; the rest I will pay before I take patent out of your or Mr. Lordner's hands."

We are the more concerned to bring to light the way and manner by which Conrad Weiser came by such a large number of acres, for various reasons. First of all, no Indian Agent seems to be above suspicion, now-a-days especially. Furthermore, it has been whispered and insinuated through taking anecdotes, at all events that our hero, too, as well as all other Indian traders, knew how to defraud poor Lo. The story which has been orally perpetuated down to the day that now is, and which ever and anon crops forth in print, touching his wily procedure, is likely to confirm one in the belief that he was not clear of stratagem. It is of this tenor: "Shekallamy came to Conrad Weiser and informed him of his glorious dream. 'I dreamed,' said Shekallamy, 'that Tarachawagon (Weiser) had presented me with a rifle.' Conrad, of course, handed over to his dusky friend the coveted weapon, suspecting all the while that Shekallamy had a dream — 'which was not all a dream.'

"A few days later Conrad Weiser had a dream, and told Shekallamy so. The Chief asked for its revelation. 'I dreamed,' said Tarachawagon, 'that Shekallamy presented me with the large and beautiful island nestled in the Susquehanna river.' The nonplussed Chief at once made over his favorite island — the Isle of Que — but added, 'Conrad, let us never dream again!'"

We believe the whole to be a mere make-up. It is true, the Isle of Que, on which a part of Selinsgrove now stands, had been owned by the old Interpreter, and that it remained for one or two generations in the possession ot his direct descendants; but there is nothing to warrant us in saying that his title rested on a mere nightly speculation. On the other hand, it is true that Shekallamy had been a very poor chief, so poor that Conrad Weiser intercedes for him, as an object of charity, before the Council at Philadelphia. It is necessary, before we may credit the story, to set aside all the testimony, volunteered from all parties of his day, in confirmation of his uprightness, probity and honor. To accept the good report which Conrad Weiser challenged for himself in his open, working day, and in the same breath, as it were, to admit that he would rob an Indian Chief, in such a wholesale manner, recommending him as a pensioner to the government besides — is absurd.

We are more ready to trust a tradition which our late father never tired of repeating, and runs thus:

"Conrad Weiser once sat resting on a log in his extensive forest land. Presently an Indian, who had stealthily approached, squatted down hard by him. Conrad moved aside somewhat; the intruder pressed harder against him. Again Conrad granted more room; but the Indian pressed still harder on him. Then Conrad demanded an explanation of his strange and rude procedure. The Indian answered: "Thus the whites did to the Indians. They lighted unbidden on our lands. We moved on; they followed. We still moved, and they still followed. We are moving onward now, and they are following after. Conrad, I will not push you from the log entirely. But will your people cease their crowding ere we roll into the waters?" This is at all events plausible. And if any of our readers desire some proof — let them look all around! This is, in Indian phrase, more than 'the singing of a bird.' It has abundant authenticity.

We have not succeeded in tracing Conrad Weiser's descendants to any satisfactory degree, either in line or locality. American life has not yet crystallized the *family*. Well grounded facts, reliable traditions and legitimate inferences, nevertheless, lead us to believe that his sons quartered themselves on their paternal grounds originally, with the design of devoting themselves to farming, and from these several centres spread over the counties of Berks, Lebanon, Northumberland, and their offspring again into Dauphin, York, Franklin, Lehigh, Montgomery and Bucks, as well as into the states of New York and Ohio. His posterity has become quite large, and in more than one instance respectable and significant.

All his sons inherited their sire's glowing patriotism and gave evidence of it during the wars of their day. One was shot through the lungs, at the battle of Brandywine, but survived. It was frequently mentioned in our hearing that the brave man never realized his wound until his boot had filled with blood. The bullet was carried with him to his grave. We cannot tell which son he was, with certainty.

Samuel, after having walked in the ways of his father for a while, both before and after Conrad's decease abandoned forever the governmental and political arena. Of his children we have learned nothing.

Philip, who is said to have been the wounded soldier, settled on that part of the inheritance on which the town of Womelsdorf now stands — the homestead. His son Jabeth succeeded him, a daughter of whom (*Mrs. Elizabeth Lewars*) [1] is now living at Hamburg, Pa. She was born June 16, 1788, and is doubtless the oldest surviving descendant of Conrad Weiser. She has in her possession a large silver spoon one hundred and fifty years old, which was one of a half dozen bought and presented to the daughter of Conrad Weiser, Mrs. Muhlenberg, as a bridal gift. [2] We are very sure of owning a mate to it: but it puzzles us greatly to account for the primisenous distribution of the set, as well as for its escape from the Muhlenberg household.

Philip was the father of another son, *Conrad,* whose family-roll we are enabled to enter in full. He raised a group of twelve, four of whom died in younger years. The surviving eight children were Benjamin, Frederick, John Conrad, Daniel, Sophia (Schawber), Hannah (Rhoads), Mary (Holstein), Catherine (Bassler). This grandson of our hero located along the Susquehanna river, in what is now Snyder county, at Selinsgrove, a part of which town had once been known as Weisersburg. The Rev. Dr. Daniel Weiser had been the latest surving member of this line. He died December 9, 1875. There are a number of grand and great-grandchildren of the third Conrad still living in that district.

The same Philip had also a third son, who bore his father's name, of whose history we are not able to record anything.

Benjamin, the youngest son of the older Conrad, seems to have inherited the greater share of his father's roving propensity. He was pursued by the phantom of recovering on his sire's possessions in the State of New York. In a letter to Governor Simon Snyder, April 2, 1788, he says in reference to the matter in prospect: "Since I saw yon last I saw a gopd deal of the world (that is, different sorts of people). I was last summer at Mohawk river, but could not get matters settled to my mind. I might have gotten a considerable sum for my right, though. I shall now, in a few days, set off again, and am sure of having it done pretty nigh to my satisfaction.' This letter had been written from Providence, one of the points along the "shore of New England," where, according to Muhlenberg's words, his grandfather had wandered prior to his last visit to Pennsylvania.

For many long years the idea of reclaiming the Schoharie lands was entertained by some of Conrad Weiser's descendants. We are glad to record, though, that the same game of 'dispossessing' the later occupants was not played on them, which caused such sorrow to the original squatters. *"Besser Unrecht zu leiden, als ungerecht zu straiten."* (See Note B at the end of Chapter.)

We have not been able to gather any notices of the other sons of Conrad Weiser, or of their posterity. *Peter* and *Frederick* can, therefore, be but mentioned.

Of the daughters we present some spare notes. The eldest, *Anna Maria,* became the wife of the honored and venerable Lutheran Patriarch, Rev. Dr. Henry Melchior Muhlenberg. The ramifications of his offspring have not been furnished us.

His second daughter, *Margaret,* became the wife of a Mr. Heintzelman, by her first marriage. Conrad Weiser, in a letter to Secretary Peters, May 19, 1705, says as much. Speaking of two Indian lads, he writes: "If you could prevail with Mr. Heintzelman, my son-in-law, for a few weeks' board with him, it would be agreeable to the lads, because my daughter is somewhat used to the Indians and understands here and there a word."

In his will he also makes mention of his grandson, Israel Heintzelman.

It appears, however, that she was left a widow before the death of her father, and that, by a second marriage, she became Mrs. Finker. As he calls her "Margaret Finker" in his testamentary instrument, it has been surmised that she had entered upon her second widowhood already prior to the demise of Conrad Weiser.

If a typographical error may not be inferred, we might fix the date of Mrs. Anna Eve Weiser's death on the 10th day of June, 1781, at the estimated age of 85 years. Her remains are presumed to lie by those of her honored husband.

With these spare and very unsatisfactory notes, touching the posterity of the subject of this memoir, we must rest content. Perhaps they may serve as an incentive, in the minds of those who are more directly interested, to train up a *Family Tree* from the roots here inserted.

Col. J, L. Stichter, of the city of Reading, the former proprietor of Conrad Weiser's homestead, now known as *'The White Store,'* addressed a letter to Col. J. Ross Snowden, Cor. Sec. of the Historical Society, September 1, 1869, from which we extract the opening lines:

CONRAD WEISER'S STORE IN READING.

"Dear Sir: Conrad Weiser figures so prominently in the Colonial Records of Pennsylvania that I thought your society would appropriate a relic from a building which he originally owned and constructed. In altering the walls of the building, which has since passed into my possession, I reserved a piece of the limestone foundation, a specimen of which I forwarded you by the Hon. Geo. Sharswood, to be deposited among the relics of your society. This building was constructed in 1751 by Conrad Weiser, and, after undergoing many changes, is now a large mercantile house, in which some of the old wall is still retained."

* * * * * * * *

The following letters are pertinent to the relic mentioned, to wit:

"Phila., Aug. 30, 1869.

"My Dear Sir: — I have to acknowledge the receipt of your favor of the 24th ult., with the accompanying relic of the Weiser House. I have to thank you for your politeness. I agree with you that the stone had better be deposited in the cabinet of the Historical Society, but it appears to me it had better been presented directly by yourself with a communication detailing such reminiscences of the house as you possess, and which would not fail to be a paper of great interest. If you address your letter to Col. J. Ross Snowden, Prothonotary of the Supreme Court and Corresponding Secretary of the Historical Society, to whom I have handed the relic, he will take great pride and pleasure in presenting it to the Society in your name.

Very truly yours,

"Geo. Sharswood.

"J. L. Stichter, Esq., Reading."

"Historical Society of Penna.,

"Phila., Sept. 2, 1869.

"My Dear Sir: — I have received your favor of yesterday, and also from Judge Sharswood the interesting relic, to which your letter refers. Any memorial of the distinguished Indian Agent and Interpreter and Soldier, Col. Weiser, possesses peculiar interest, more especially so valuable a relic as a piece of the foundation stone of his mansion house in Reading, built in 1751. This relic will be placed among the cherished objects of interest in the cabinet of our Society. I will have the honor to present it, in your behalf, at the next meeting of our Society, and will then read your interesting account of Col. Weiser and have it placed among our archives.

"I am with great respect

"Your obedient servant,

"James Ross Snowden, Corres. Sec.

"J. L. Stichter, Esq., Reading, Pa."

"Historical Society of Penna.,

"Phila., Sept. 14, 1869.

"Sir: — I am directed by the Society to communicate to you their thanks for a piece of the limestone foundation of the mansion originally constructed and owned by Conrad Weiser, a German refugee. This venerable relic will be placed in our cabinet of curiosities, and your interesting letter will be filed among the archives of our Society.

"I have the honor to be

"Your obedient servant,

"James Shrigley, Librarian,

"J. L. Stichter, Esq., Reading, Pa."

Note A. — Mrs. Lewars, the aged grandaughter of Conrad Weiser, tenaciously held to the opinion that the old Interpreter had another daughter, Elizabeth, who had been intermarried with the Reverend Mr. Schultze. We have found no confirmation of her saying in any record extant, but are quite willing to credit her report. She also related that still another daughter had been intermarried with a Mr. Womelsdorf, to whom the father gave the farm upon which the town of Womelsdorf now stands — he having located and named the town.

We have not the mind to dispute with a witness of her age and ancestral line. We are the less inclined to controvert the sayings of Conrad Weiser's descendants so long as there is no direct antagonism with known fact, on account of the imperfection of the records at hand. Thus, for instance, .Mrs. Muhlenberg is written "Anna Maria" here, and simply "Anna" in another place, whilst "Maria" stands for a sister. So, too, we find the names "Magdalena" and "Margretta" used interchangeably, sometimes indicating one, then again two daughters.

Note B. — Repeated attempts were made at different times to investigate the titles and papers relative to those New York lands. Attorney Miller was on one occasion employed to enter upon the task of dispossessing the occupants. The aggressive party was led to entertain great hope of success. Finally it was discovered that rats had carried away the records. A happy ratification, say we.

[1] See Note A. Mrs. L. has since died.
[2] We are indebted for these particulars to the late Rev. W. F. P. Davis, of Reading, Pa.

Chapter Nineteen - Summary and Conclusion

Having reached the end of our task, we may be allowed to rest and look back upon the course we have followed; and, like him who has journeyed awhile, sit down at the end of our way and ask for the result obtained from our efforts.

Our way has not been like the path-finder's, which must first be discovered and then trodden with difficulty and caution. It lay not unmarked over a trackless region, but broken, open and well beaten by Conrad Weiser himself. Even a century and a decade of years could not close it over again — so long did it retain the 'right of way.' He made his own history, and we had but to follow in his

"Footprints on the sands of time."

Like every noble soul, he proved his own biographer, and, accordingly, rendered it an easy task for the scribe coming after to perform the part of a recorder and chronicler. Man and the race make history, indeed, but not so much with pen and parchments as by the weaving of noble deeds into a living, harmonious whole. The unbroken chain which Conrad Weiser forged in the furnace of his trying life, we simply recounted, link by link, from his cradle to his tomb. And the fact that the history of a mortal may thus be detailed, a hundred and more years after he has passed by and away, without indulging in verbose panegyrics or amplifying eulogy, — *this* shows that we have not been walking side by side with a myth, but with a character worthy of a record. We protest against the charge of having galvanized a fictitious skeleton into an apparent life. We continued with a still living man, though dead. Live men cannot die. We bury only dead men. As there are men dead, though they live, so are there men living, though they are dead. The dead bury the dead, whilst the living hold the living in life everlasting. In a certain sense, he that liveth shall never die.

We set out in search of Conrad Reiser's ancestry, in Gross-Aspach, in Herrenburg, and followed his sire to Afsttedt, in Backnang — his birthplace. We saw him borne a babe in his mother's arms to the church at Kueppingen, where he was christened *"John Conrad."* We flitted with the family of five children back to the town of Gross-Aspach, where his excellent mother died. We accompanied the motherless household in its sad exodus from the fated "Vaterland" to London, and stood near to them in their sufferings and want along the Blackmoor with the Indian Chiefs. Thence we sailed with them on a six months' voyage to New York. We related the days of trial on Livingston Manor and Schoharie Valley. Whilst the sire stood as helmsman to the Palatinate Colony there, we trailed off with the son, for several months, among the Maqua Indians, and saw him there laying the foundation to his future mission. During the father's efforts, successes and reverses, we beheld the son growing into manhood, entering into marriage, and succeeding the elder in the office of benefactor to German and English, to Indian and white men. Following the eventful life of the sire down to his pitiable end, we related his offspring's arrival at Tulpehocken, in Pennsylvania. Here there remained for us to toll the interesting story of thirty years — how he emerged into prominence as a citizen, leader and officer; serving his day, his people and his country, as Justice, Colonel and Chief of the Indian Bureau. We stood by his tomb as we stood by his cradle.

Nor did we forget to relate his intimate relation to God during his long and constant contact with his fellow men. In a word, we presented the record of his own writing — crowded with thoughts, words and deeds that breathed, lived and fruited in a glowing immortality.

And now it remains but for us, briefly, to learn some lessons from Conrad Weiser's busy life:

1. We cannot all be like him. We would not if we could. The way to fill a man with unrest, is to point out a character as an exemplar and advocate an imitation process. No two men are alike, and, consequently, their missions neither. Know thyself first, and mature *thyself* subsequently — that is a true and practical philosophy. *"Be thyself"* is a motto that is overlooked and neglected too much by far. But remembering *that,* our hero may prove the truth of Longfellow's words for us:

"Lives of great men all remind us
We can make our lives sublime,
And, departing, leave behind us
Footprints on the sands of time."

2. Goethe says: "On due reflection I am of the conviction more and more that *energy* constitutes the great difference between men." Given a good constitution and a sound mind, we believe the doctrine will realize itself in every individual. It failed not in the history of our hero. Action, perseverance, diligence, application — all these fruits of energy are manifest at every point of his life,

"Let us, then, be up and doing,
  With a heart for any fate:
  Still achieving, still pursuing,
  Learn to labor and to wait."

3. Religion is no hindrance to an earnest, active and successful life. Conrad Weiser was erratic in his piety; but this was, perhaps, more the fault of his surroundings than his own. Times and circumstances divert men from the narrow way too often. He reeled and staggered to and fro, but never abandoned his love for God and man. An old descendant says: "In those times they had no churches. Conrad Weiser was an intelligent man, and was often called on to preach funeral sermons, offer prayers, and lead in singing hymns over the burying of the dead. His son-in-law, Muhlenberg, relieved him of such duties after his arrival." How silly the notion, then, that the prosecution of one's religious duties enervates us for the discharge of our secular duties. *Ora et Labora* was finely illustrated in his long and efficient course.

"Act, act in the living present!
  Heart within and Gud o'erhead!

4. Conrad Weiser was a 'father' of the so-called "*Pennsylvania Germans*," We mention this fact as an incentive to the numerous youths in East Pennsylvania, who may consider it an affliction to find that such blood courses in their veins. Let it be remembered and repeated that our ancestry numbers, in its line, noble characters — men who would grace any position in life. Here is a pioneer in civilization, an honorable and honored public office, an historical character abreast with the men of his day — and a Pennsylvania German notwithstanding. As such he has left

"Footprints that perhaps another,
  Sailing o'er life's solemn main,
  A forlorn and shipwrecked brother,
  Seeing, shall take heart again."

Appendix

Authentic Autobiography of Conrad Weiser

[Among the several copies of Conrad Weiser's "Manuscript Autobiography," which are with his descendants, some are imperfect, and others are incorrect, in consequence of wrong translation, misconception and carelessness. We will present a reprint of the fullest and most reliable narrative, from his own hand. It has been translated for the "Collections of the Pennsylvania Historical Society," by Dr. H. H. Muhlenberg, of Reading.]

In the year 1696, on the 2d of November, I, Conrad Weiser, was born in Europe, in the land of Würtemberg, in the county (Amt) of Herrenberg, the village is called Astaet, and was christened at Kupingen, near by, as my father has informed me. I say, I was born on the second day of November, sixteen hundred and ninety-six. My father's name was John Conrad Weiser, and my mother's name was Anna Magdalena, her family name was Uebelen. My grandfather was Jacob Weiser, my great-grandfather also Jacob Weiser. He was magistrate (Schultheiss) in the village of Great Aspach, in the county (Amt) of Backnang, also in the land of Würtemberg. In this latter village my ancestors from time immemorial were born, and are buried there as well on my father's as my mother's side. In the year 1709 my mother passed into eternity on the first day of May, in the 43d year of her age, while pregnant with her sixteenth child, having children, Catrina, Margareta, Magdalena, Sabina, Conrad, George Frederick, Christopher, Barbara, John Frederick, and was buried there by the side of my ancestors. She was a woman fearing God, and much beloved by her neighbors. Her motto was, "Jesus Christ, I live for Thee, I die for Thee, Thine am I in life and death."

In the year above mentioned, namely in 1709, my father moved away from Great Aspach on the 24th of June, and took eight children with him. My eldest sister, Catrina, remained there with her husband, Conrad Boss, with whom she had two children. My father sold them his house, fields, meadows, vineyard and garden, but they could only pay him 75 gulden, the remainder, 600 gulden, was to be paid to my father at a subsequent period, which was never done, so it was made a present to them. In about two months we reached London in England, along with several thousand Germans, whom Queen Anne, of glorious remembrance, received and furnished with food. About Christmas Day we embarked, and ten ship loads with about 4,000 souls were sent to America.

On the 13th of June, 1710, we came to anelior at New York in North America, and in the same autnnm were taken to Livingston's Manor at the expense of the Queen. Here in Livingston's, or as it was called by the Germans, Loewenstein's Manor, we were to burn tar, and cultivate hemp, to repay the expenses incurred by the Queen in bringing us from Holland to England, and from England to New York. We were directed by several commissioners, viz., John Cast, Henry Mayer, Richard Seykott, (more properly Sacket), who were put in authority over his by Robert Hunter, Governor of New York. But neither object succeeded, and in the year 1713 the people were discharged from their engagements and declared free. Then the people scattered themselves over the whole Province of New York. Many remained where they were. Abont 150 families determined to remove to Schochary (a place about forty English miles to the west of Albany.) They therefore sent in July deputies to the land of the Maquas to consult with the Indians about it, who allowed them to occupy Schochary. For the Indian deputies who were it England at the time the German people were lying in tents on the Blackmoor, had made a present to Queen Anne of this Schochary, that she might settle these people upon it. Indian guides were sent to show the Germans where Schochary was. My father was the first of the German deputies.

In November, 1713, when the above mentioned deputies had returned from the Maqua country to Livingston's Manor, the people moved the same autumn to Albany and Schenectady, so as to be able to move in the spring to Schochary. Bread was very dear, but the people worked very hard for a living, and the old settlers were very kind and did much good to the Germans, although some of a different disposition were not wanting. My father reached Schenectady the same fall, where he remained with his family over winter with a man named John Meyndert.

A chief of the Maqua nation named Quagnant visited my father, and they agreed that I should go with Quagnant into his country to learn the Maqua language. I accompanied him and reached the Maqua country in the latter end of November and lived with the Indians: here I suffered much from the excessive cold, for I was but badly clothed, and towards spring also from hunger, for the Indians had nothing to eat. A bushel of Indian corn was worth five to six shillings. And at this period the Indians, when drunk, were so barbarous, that I was frequently obliged to hide from drunken Indians.

1714. In the spring, my father removed from Schenectady to Schochary, with about 100 families in great poverty. One borrowed a horse here, another there, also a cow and plow harness. With these things they united and broke up jointly so much land that they raised nearly enough corn for their own consumption the following year. But this year they suffered much from hunger, and made many meals on the wild potatoes and ground beans which grew in great abundance at that place. The Indians called the potatoes *Ochna-nada,* the ground beans *Otach-Raquara.* When we wished for meal, we had to travel 35 to 40 miles to get it, and had then to borrow it on credit. They would get a bushel of wheat here, a couple at another place, and were often absent from home three or four days before they could reach their suffering wives and children crying for bread.

The people had settled in villages, of which there were seven. The first and nearest to Schenectady was called Kneskern-dorf; 2. Gerlachs-dorf: 3. Fuchsen-dorf: 4. Hans George Schmidts-dorf; 5. Weisers-dorf, or Brunnen-dorf; 6. Hartmans-dorf; 7. Ober Weisers-dorf. So named after the deputies who were sent from Livingston's Manor to the Maqua country.

Towards the end of July I returned from among the Indians to my father, and had made considerable progress, or had learned the greater part of the Macpia language. An English mile from my father's house there living several Macpia families, and there were always Mannas among us luuitiiig, so that there was always something for me to do in interpreting, bnt without pay. There was no one else to be found among our people who understood the language, so that I gradually became completely master of the language, so far as my years and other circumstances permitted.

Here now this people lived peaceably for several years without preachers or magistrates. Each one did as he thought proper. About this time I became very sick and expected to die, and was willing to die, for my stepmother was indeed a step-mother to me. By her influence my father treated me very harshly; I had no other friend, and had to bear hunger and cold. I often thought of running away, but the sickness mentioned put a bit in my mouth; I was bound as if by a rope to remain with my father to obey him.

I have already mentioned that my father was a widower when he left Germany, and landed in 1710 with eight children, in New York, where my two brothers, George Frederick and Christopher, were bound by the Governor, with my then sick father's consent, over to Long Island. The following winter my youngest brother, John Frederick, died in the sixth year of his age, and was buried in Livingston's *bush,* as the expression then was, and was the first one buried where now the Reformed church in Weisersdorf stands.

In the year 1711 my father married my step-mother, whom I have mentioned above. It was an unhappy match, and was the cause of my brothers and sisters all becoming scattered. At last I was the only one left at home, except the three children he had by my step-mother, viz., John Frederick, Jacob and Rebecca. Everything went crab-fashion; one misfortune after another happened to our family, of which I always was partaker. I frequently did not know where to turn, and learned to pray to God, and the Bible became a very agreeable book to me.

But to return to Schochary. The people had taken possession without informing the governor of New York, who, after letting them know his dissatisfartion, sold the land to seven rich merehants, four of whom HvimI in Albany, the other three in New York. The names of those in Albany were Myndert Shvller, John Shvller, Robert Livingston, Peter Van Brughen; of those in New York were George Clarke, at that time Secretary, Doctor Stadts, Rip Van Dam. Upon this a great uproar arose in Schochary and Albany, because many persons in Albany wished the poor people to return their lands. The people of Schochary divided into two parties; the strongest did not wish to obey, but to keep the land, and therefore sent deputies to England to obtain a grant from George the first, not only for Schochary, but for more land in addition. But the plans did not succeed according to their wishes, for in the first place the deputies had to leave secretly and embarked at Philadelphia in 1718. As soon as they got to sea they fell into the hands of pirates, who robbed them as well as the crew of their money, but then set them free.

My father, who was one of the deputies, was three times tied up and flogged, but would not confess to having money; finally William Scheff, the other deputy, said to the pirates, this man and I have a purse in common, and I have already given it to you, he has nothing to give you; upon which they let him go free. The ship had to put into Boston to purchase necessaries for the crew and passengers, in place of those taken by the pirates. When they reached England, they found times had changed ami that there was no longer a Queen Anne on the throne. They still found some of the old friends and advocates of the Germans, among whom were the Chaplains at the King's German Chapel, Messrs. Boehm and Roberts, who did all in their power. The affairs of the deputies finally reached the Lords Commissioners of Trade and Plantations, and the Governor of New York, Robert Hunter, was called home. In the meanwhile the deputies got into debt; Walrath, the third deputy, became homesick, and embarked on a vessel bound to New York, but died at sea. The other two were thrown into prison; they wrote in time for money, but owing to the ignorance and overconfidence of the persons who had the money to transmit which the people had collected, it reached England very slowly. In the meantime Robert Hunter had arrived in England, had arranged the sale of the Schochary lands in his own way before the Board of Trade and Plantations. The opposite party was in prison, without friends or money. Finally, when a bill of exchange for seventy pounds sterling arrived, they were released from prison, petitioned anew, and in the end got an order to the newly arrived Governor of New York, William Burnet, to grant vacant land to the Germans who had been sent to New York by the deceased Queen Anne.

Towards the end of the year 1720 this William Burnet arrived in New York. In the commencement of the year 1721 I was sent to New York with a petition to Governor Burnet. He appeared friendly, and stated what kind of an order from the Lords of Trade and Plantations he brought with him, which he was resolved to comply with, but deputies were yet in England, not content with the decision, but could get nothing more done. In the last named year, viz., 1721, William Scheff returned home, having quarreled with my father; they hath had hard heads. At last, in the month of November, 1723, my father also returned. Scheff died six weeks after his return.

Governor Burnet gave patents for land to the few who were willing to settle in the Maqua eountry, namely in Stone Arabia, and above the falls, [1] but none on the river, as the people hoped. They therefore scattered, the larger part removed to the Maqua country or remained in Schochary, and bought the land from the before named rich men.

The people got news of the land on the *Swatara* and *Tulpehocken,* in Pennsylvania; many of them united and cut a road from Schochary to the Susquehanna river, carried their goods there, and made canoes, and floated down the river to the mouth of the Swatara creek, and drove their cattle over land. This happened in the spring of the year 1723. From there they came to Tulpehocken, and this was the beginning of Tulpehoeken settlement. Others followed this party and settled there, at first, also, without the permission of the Proprietary of Pennsylvania or his Commissioners; also against the consent of the Indians, from whom the land had not yet been purchased. There was no one among the people to govern them, each one did as he pleased, and their obstinacy has stood in their way ever since. Here I will leave them for a time, and describe my own circumstances.

In 1720, while my father was in England, I married my Ann Eve, and was given her in marriage by the Rev. John Frederick Heger, Reformed clergyman, on the 22d of November, in my father's house in Schochary.

In 1722, the 7th of September, my son Philip was born, and was baptized by John Bernhard von Duehren, Lntheran clergyman; his sponsors were Philip Brown and wife.

The 13th of January, 1725, my daughter Anna Madlina was born; was baptized by John Jacob Oehl, Reformed clergyman; her sponsors were Christian Bauch, Junior, and my sister Barbara.

In 1727, my daughter Maria was born on the 24th of June, and was baptized by William Christopher Birkenmeyer, Lutheran clergyman. Her sponsors were Niklas Feg and wife.

In 1728, December 24th, my son Frederick was born; was baptized by John Bernhart von Duehren, Lutheran clergyman; his sponsors were Niklas Feg and wife.

These four were born to me at Schochary. *Afterwards, namely, in 1729, I removed to Pennsylvania,* and settled in Tulpehocken, where the following children were born to me, namely:

1730, the 27th of February, my son Peter was born, and in 1731, the 15th of February, I had two sons born, who were called Christopher and Jacob; the first lived 15 weeks, the latter 13 weeks, when they were released from the evils of this world and taken to a happy eternity.

1732, June 19th, my daughter Elizabeth was born.

1734, the 28th of January, my daughter Margaret was born.

The 23d of April, 1735, my son Samuel was born.

The 18th of July, 1736, I had again a son born to me. I called him Benjamin; when he was three months old, the care of the Almighty God took him away; the same year my daughter Elizabeth followed him. A merciful God will give them all to nie again, to the honor of His glory.

The 11th of August, 1740, another son was born; I called his name Jaebez. the mercy of God removed him from the evil of these days when he was 17 days old.

The 27th of February, 1742, another daughter was born; I called her name Hanna; the following 11th of August she went into a happy eternity.

The 16th of March of this year my dear daughter Madlina went from time to eternity, through an easy death, after a long and tedious illness. Her faith, consolation and refuge was in the crucified Savior, Jesus Christ, whom she had vowed herself to in days of health, with soul and body.

The 12th of August, 1744, my son Benjamin was born.

[1] The falls of the Mohawk river.

Letter of Conrad Weiser

To The Leaders at Ephrata, September 3, 1743.

[This letter was found among the papers of the late I. Daniel Rupp, the well-known historian of Pennsylvania. It is interesting and important, because it clears up a point in the life of Conrad Weiser which had been obscure thus far. In May, 1735, he joined the Seventh Day Baptists at Ephrata with Rev. John Peter Miller and nine other families of Tulpehocken. It was known that he withdrew from the sect at a later period, but the exact time and the reasons which induced him to take this step were unknown. Both are now supplied by this new letter, by which he severed his connection with the Ephrata brethren. — W. J. Hinke.]

Worthy and Dear Friends and Brethren

It cannot be denied at Ephrata that I and several other members of the community, partly gone to their rest, partly still living, were compelled to protest for a considerable time against the domination of conscience, the suppression of innocent minds, against the prevailing pomp and luxury, both in dress and magnificent buildings, but we achieved about as much as nothing; on the contrary, in spite of all protests, this practice was still more eagerly continued, and following the manner of the world, the attempt was made to cover such pride and luxury with the name of God. It was most zealously defended, so that for years nothing has been heard in picnic assemblies but the boast: *"There the work stands; it is the work of God,"* as if it were the first Babylonian masterpiece. Whole assemblies were held in honor of this loathsome idolatry, while the leaders have indulged in the most fulsome self-praise by all kinds of fictitious stories.

For these and other reasons, which I reserve for myself to state them at a fitting opportunity, I take leave of your young, but already decrepit sect, and I desire henceforth to be treated as a stranger, especially by the the presiding officers (superintendents), whenever should come to Ephrata because of business or other personal inclinations, or should meet you somewhere else. You will no doubt know how to instruct, as usual, the other, partly innocent, minds, as to what they have to consider me. I make a distinction between them and you, and hope the time will come when they shall be liberated from their physical and spiritual bondage, as also from the thraldom of conscience, under which they are groaning. I protest once more against you, the overseers, who teeil yourselves and do not spare the Hock, but scatter and devour them.

****

*** [A few lines are here torn off.] ***

****

I hope the end is near and the deliverance has come. Of course I know beforehand that you will not consider my words, especially since I am not the son of a prophet or a prophet myself nor do I appeal to a spirit in my head or body as the cause of this letter, put my conclusions are founded upon the eternal truth and the reasonableness of the thing itself. I am in earnest; you may ridicule me as much as you please.

Herewith I conclude and live in hope that the time will come when all knees shall bow before the name of Jesus, even those of such proud saints who publicly declare rather to burn in hell than bow before Him.

Why doest thou extol thyself, O poor earth? The judgment of God can humble thee in a moment. Do it rather willingly; it is no disgrace, for the heathen are his inheritance and the uttermost parts of the earth his possession. He is a King of all kings and a Lord of all lords. Worship, majesty and power belong to Him, for the Father has made all things subject to Him. He will give His honor to no other, nor His glory to the mighty. He is the Lord, and beside Him there is no Savior.

If there is any one not satisfied with my statement, let him convince me of the contrary. Victory belongs to truth. The authority of man has no power. To be silent is good at times, but in this case it would be bad. If you have anything to say in your defence, or undertaken a reformation, let me know, for I shall be glad to hear it.

Finally, I remain a friend of truth and sincerity, and of all those who love them, but a sworn enemy of all lies and hypocrisy. Farewell.

September 3, 1743.   Conrad Weiser.

Dedication Hymn

Conrad Weiser composed the following beautiful hymns which were used at the dedication of a church:

Jehovah, Herr und Majestaet!
Hoer unser kindlieh Flehen:
Neig deine Ohren zum Gebet
Der Schaaren, die da stehen
Vor deinem heiligen Angesicht:
Verschmaehe unsere Bitte nicht,
Um deines Namens willen!

Dies Hans wird hente eingeweiht
Vou deinem Bundes-Volke:
Lasz uns, Herr, deine Herrlichkeit
Hernieder in der Wolke,
Dasz sie erfuelle dieses Haus
Und treibe alles Boese aus,
Um deines Namens willen!

Es halte Niemand das gemein,
Was du fuer rein erklaeret:
Dies Hans soil eine Wohnung sein,
Worin man dich verehret.
Es bleibe stets ein Heiligthum
Fuer's reine Evangelium!
Um deines Namens willen!

Verleihe, dasz es nie gebricht
An treuen Kirchen-Raethen,
Die nach Gewissen, Amt und Plificht
Fuer sich und Andere beten,
Damit durch ihren Dienst und Treu
Der Kirche wohlgerathen sei,
Um deines Namens willen!

O Majestaet, erzuerne nicht,
Dasz wir uns unterwinden,
Zu bitten, dasz dein Recht und Licht
Hier stetig sei zu finden!
Drum gieb uns Lelirer, die erfuellt
Mit deinem Geist und Ebenbild,
Urn deines Namens willen!

Wenn deine treuen Knechte hier
In deinem Namen lehren,
Wenn sie erhoehen dein Panier;
Dann lasz dein Volk so hoeren,
Dasz sich eroeffne ihr Verstand,
Ihr Wille werde umgewandt,
Um deines Namens willen!

Hier oeffne sich der Boten Mund,
Und triefe recht vom Fette!
Er mache Fluch und Segen kund,
Und ringe in die Wette
Mit Gott und seines Geistes Kraft,
Die ihm den Weg zum Herzen schafft,
Um Jesu Christi willen!

Lasz, Jesu, diese Quelle sein
Ein reines Meer der Gnaden,
Darinnen unsere Kindelein
Von Erb- und Suenden-Schaden
Durch dein Verdienst, Blut, Schweisz und Tod
Errettet werde aus der Noth,
Um deines Namens Willen!

Lasz, Majestaet, auf diesem Platz
Die reinste Lehre bleiben,
Und deine Knechte solchen Schatz
Nach deinem Willen treiben.
Behuete uns vor Zaenkerei,
Vor Sicherheit und Heuchelei,
Um deines Namens willen!

Das ist und bleibet ewig wahr,
Was Christi Mund gesprochen:
Wer ab- und zuthut, hat ganz klar

Des Mittlers Wort gebrochen.
Drum irret nicht, Gott laesset sich
In solcher Sache absonderlich
Nicht in die Laenge spotten!

Lasz dieses Hans die Werkstatt sein,
Worinn viel tausend Seelen
In Busz nnd Glauben nur allein
Mit Jesu sich vermaehlen
Durch deines Wurtes Lebens-Saft
Und deiner Sakramenten Kraft,
Uni deines Namens willen!

Gieb endlich, hoechste Majestaet
Des Himmels und der Erden,
Dasz Fuerbitt, Dank, Preis und Gebet
Mag hier geopfert werden
Fuer jeden Stand der Christenheit,
Damit in alle Ewigkeit
Dein Nam' geehret werde!

Vor Feuer, Krieg und Wassers-Noth
Wollst du dies haus bewahren!
Damit nach sel'gem Tod
Die Nachkommen erfahren,
Dasz wir dich, wahren Gott, geliebt
Und uns in deinem Wort genebt,
Um deines Namens willen!

The Story of Regina

One of the most thrilling stories connected with the time of Conrad Weiser is that of a young girl named Retina Hartman. It occurred during the cruel French and Indian war, which continued from 1755 to 1763.

The colonies inhabited by the German immigrants belonged to England, whilst the French possessed Canada and Louisiana. A war broke out between England and France, and this war was extended to the American continent. The French succeeded in gaining the Indians to their side. It is believed that the French promised to repossess the Indians of the lands which they formerly occupied and which were then in the possession of the Germans. The result was that the savage Indians fought for the French, and, returning to Berks county, committed numerous cruelties and outrages. The Germans, who were without protection, were often surprised by the savages, and many of them scalped and killed, and their homes burned. In a number of places the men always took their rifles with them to church, and some of them stood on guard outside, whilst the people worshiped inside. The history of Berks county abounds with Indian cruelties. In many cases the children who were not killed, were carried oif into captivity. The people of the whole county, especially the northern part, were for years in a state of insecurity, and their sufferings were great. The story given below is only one of many similar ones.

Among the Palatinate fanatics who had emigrated to the Tulpehocken region to enjoy religious freedom was that of Henry Hartman, which consisted of father, mother, two sons and two danghters. They resided in what is now Bethel township, uear the place where Fort Henry was afterwards erected. The parents were pious people, who taught their children to pray, read the Scriptures and to sing. There were of course no Sunday schools, and about the only instruction which the children reeeived came from the parents. But this instruction was of the right sort, as is evident from the fruit it bore. The family could attend church but seldom, the only church at Tidpehocken being a considerable distance away. One of the favorite hymns often suno; by the family commenced thus: "Alone, yet not alone am I." This hymn was a source of consolation to them in their lonely home, it proved a great blessing after awhile, as we shall see.

On October 16, 1755, the Hartman family were visited by a terrible tragedy. The mother and youngest son had gone to the mill. During their absence the cruel Indians had surprised the family and performed their bloody work. When the mother and son returned, they found that the father and the oldest son had been murdered and scalped by the Indians, and the two daughters, Barbara, twelve years of age, and Regina, ten years of age, taken captives, and the buildings burned! What an awful sight! What a fearful change, the work of a few minutes! The once happy family was partly murdered. partly captured, and the remainder homeless. What must have been the feelings of the mother and daughter? And what must have been the feelings of the two innocent daughters, as they beheld their father and brother murdered in cold blood, and the torch applied to the beloved humble home, whilst they themselves were about being carried away into unknown regions, with rude and cruel Indians as their only companions. They could hardly hope ever to see their mother and brother again.

The two sisters were taken to an obscure place in the mountain and held there until a number of child captives had been collected, when they entered upon their journey. Many were too young to walk, and these were tied on the backs of the older and stronger ones. Their journey led them through woods and briers, and over rough, stony paths. Their clothing was nearly all torn off their bodies. Thus they traveled several hundred miles. Then Barbara was separated from Regina. This was a most painful experience for both. Their hearts were still bleeding from the loss of their parents and their home, and now they were parted without any hope of ever meeting again in this world. And they never saw each other again. Here the record ends as far as Barbara is concerned. Nothing is known of her subsequent experience and history. It is assumed that she died as a captive.

Regina was taken about one hundred miles farther, where she and a little girl, which she had to carry, were given in charge of a cruel Indian woman, who had a son. Her experience can better be imagined than described. It was hard enough to be deprived of parents and home, but this was not all. The son was often away from home for long periods, and poor Regina was compelled, under threats of death, to secure the food upon which they subsisted. Conrad Weiser stated that when he resided in New York they often made a meal on "wild potatoes and ground beans, which grew in abundance." These no doubt furnished food for the Indians of New York, among whom Regina is supposed to have been at this time.

The condition and surroundings of the young and tender-hearted Regina were most sad. From ten to nineteen years of age, when she mostly needed the care of parents and friends, slie was compelled to live beyond the pale of civilization and among savage Indians. Her native tongue was German, but during these years she never heard a word of German except in conversation with her younger companion, who was brought with her into captivity. She gradually became reconciled to her sad fate, became inured to the life of the Indians, adopted their customs and learned their language. Thus she spent the nine years of her exile without any hope of being restored to her mother.

The cruel war continued and numerous nnirders were committed in Berks county. However, by 1760 the Indians and the French were finally defeated and driven from this part of the country. When the treaty of peace was made, Col. Bouquet, who commanded the English army, included in the treaty a condition that all the children who had been taken captive during the war should be returned. They were accordingly gathered from different sections and brought to Fort Duquesne, where the city of Pittsburg is now located. They were ragged, and some of them were almost entirely without clothing. Their sufferings must have been great, for it was in the month of December. The garrison of the fort supplied the poor captives with clothing as far as possible.

The captive children were then brought to Carlisle, Pa., and notice published in the papers that parents whose children had been taken captive during the war, should come and claim them. The heart of Mrs. Hartman was filled with joy, because she hoped that now at last her long lost daughters would be returned to her. She went to Carlisle, but how should she recognize her children? During these nine years they had greatly changed, not only by time, but especially by their condition. The unfavorable surroundings naturally had their effects upon the young girls. But the mother hoped and prayed.

We now come to the most touching and thrilling part of the story. The children were drawn up in line, and the anxious mother walked along the line and looked carefully at each child, but reached the end without finding either Barbara or Regina. We may imagine her feeling of disappointment. Col. Bouquet asked the mother whether the children had no marks on their bodies by which she could recognize them, or whether she could not do something by which they might recognize her. The mother replied that they used to sing certain hymns in the family, before the children were taken captive, and possibly they might still remember these. Col. Bouquet asked her to sing one of these hymns. With trembling voice the troubled mother commenced to sing:

Allein und doch nicht ganz alleine,
   Bin ich in meiner Einsamkeit;
Denn wenn ich ganz verlassen scheine,
   Vertreibt mir Jesus selbst die Zeit;
Ich bin bei Ihm und Er bei mir,
   So kommt mir gar nichts einsam fuer.

The following is a translation:

Alone, yet not alone am I,
  Though in this solitude so drear;
I feel my Savior always nigh,
  He comes the weary hours to cheer;
I am with Him and He with me,
  Even here alone I cannot be.

The mother had scarcely sung two lines, when Regina sprang from the line, joined in singing the old familiar hymn, and mother and daughter embraced each other and shed tears of joy that they were united again after a dreary separation of nine years. Their joy was marred only by the fact that Barbara was not there. Regina had never heard of her since their separation soon after their capture. She was never heard of again. When Regina and her mother were about leaving, Regina's companion clung to her and begged to be permitted to go with her. The record implies that her request was granted, and that she was brought along to Tulpehocken.

Truly, "godliness is profitable unto all things." The devotional spirit of the Hartman family brought its own reward in the discovery of the lost daughter. But for the singing of the familiar hymn, the mother and daughter would likely never have found each other. It is an interesting fact that the hymn, by the singing of which Regina recognized her mother, describes her feelings during her captivity most aptly. The good seed sown in child hearts will bear fruit in after years. The religious instruction imparted to the child Regina was not lost. It is stated that during her captivity she often took her young German companion away from the Indian hut to some secluded spot and engaged in prayer with her, and in singing the hymns which she had learned under the parental roof. Again, when Regina returned to the home of her mother, she inquired for the family Bible and the old hymn book. Dr. Henry Melchior Muhlenberg, the celebrated Lutheran patriarch, states in his official report that the mother told him that Regina often asked for "the book in which Christ so kindly spoke to the children, and the people could speak to Him."

Alas, the dear old family Bible had been burned when the Indians destroyed the home. But Dr. Muhlenberg gave them a Bible and money to purchase a hymn book.

We are not told much of the history of Mrs. Hartman and her daughter Regina after the latter's return from captivity. It is assumed that they spent the remainder of their lives in Tulpehocken. Dr. Muhlenberg knew the family well. From him we learn the birthplaces of father and mother in Germany. He also gives us the motive of their coming to the new world. Like many others they sought a country of religious freedom. Dr. M. says that "the father was already old and too weak to do hard work, but endeavored to bring up his children in the fear of God in this land, where few schools were to be found." Regina lived to a good age, and was a pious lady. She was buried by the side of her mother at Christ Lutheran Church, near Stouchsburg, Pa.

This is, in short, the story of Regina, which has such a large place in the hearts of our Pennsylvania German people.

www.ingramcontent.com/pod-product-compliance
Lightning Source LLC
Chambersburg PA
CBHW031524040426

42445CB00009B/384